The Macmillan Book of
THE HUMAN BODY

The Macmillan Book of
THE HUMAN BODY

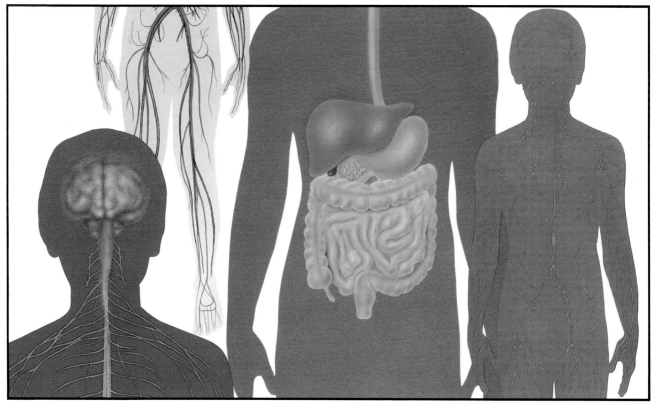

BY MARY ELTING / ILLUSTRATED BY KIRK MOLDOFF

MACMILLAN PUBLISHING COMPANY • New York
COLLIER MACMILLAN PUBLISHERS • London

ACKNOWLEDGMENTS

Every author of a book about the human body must read books written by scientists, teachers, and researchers. There are thousands of such volumes that tell how people are born and grow and do the things they do. Probably no one person could read all of them, but to the many writers whose books I have consulted I owe thanks. I am especially grateful to Helena Curtis whose *Biology: The Science of Life* guided my explorations. My special thanks go also to Elisabeth Kandel, M.D., who was kind enough to read and check my manuscript. Judy Minger, who introduces first graders to the body's wonders, gave me valuable advice, and so did Rosanna Hansen and Elaine Israel, my patient and helpful editors. To them, too, warm thanks.

MARY ELTING

Macmillan Publishing Company
866 Third Avenue, New York, NY 10022
Collier Macmillan Canada, Inc.

Printed and bound in Singapore
10 9 8 7 6 5 4 3 2 1

Designed by Antler & Baldwin, Inc.
The text of this book is set in Memphis Light.
The illustrations are acrylic and watercolor and reproduced in full color.

Library of Congress Cataloging in Publication Data

Elting, Mary, date.
The Macmillan book of the human body.
Includes index.
Summary: Describes the physical characteristics and functions of the various parts of the body.
1. Body, Human—Juvenile literature. 2. Human physiology—Juvenile literature. 3. Anatomy, Human—Juvenile literature. [1. Body, Human. 2. Human physiology. 3. Anatomy, Human] I. Title. [DNLM: 1. Anatomy—popular works. QS 4 E5lm]
QP37. E484   1986   612   85-24204
ISBN 0-02-733440-6

Contents

Your Body Around the Clock

Do you have a hard time waking up? Or are you like a rooster, ready to crow before others get out of bed?

Either way, your body is following a rhythm of its own. Some people are always woken up early by their own built-in "clock." Others can even say, "I'll wake up at 6:30." And at that exact minute, their sleep ends.

Almost everything that goes on in your body is timed in some way, as if by clockwork. Of course, the clocks aren't something you can see. It is still not clear what makes them "tick." But scientists do know that all day and all night long, your body follows certain rhythms that begin and end on time. Your temperature goes down at night, then climbs back up in the morning. This happens even if you stay awake all night. Your heartbeat gets faster as the day goes on, then slows down while you are asleep. Even though you like breakfast, your food tastes better at the end of the day. Music sounds louder in the evening. Your sense of smell is sharper then, too.

Teachers have noticed that most young people have a rhythm in their activity. As if a timekeeper is giving signals, students are restless for about half an hour, then quiet down and concentrate on their books for half an hour. Most people's brains seem to do the best work between 1 P.M. and 4 P.M.

Sleep is also an important part of your body's daily rhythms. By the time you are seventy-five years old, you will have spent about twenty-five years asleep!

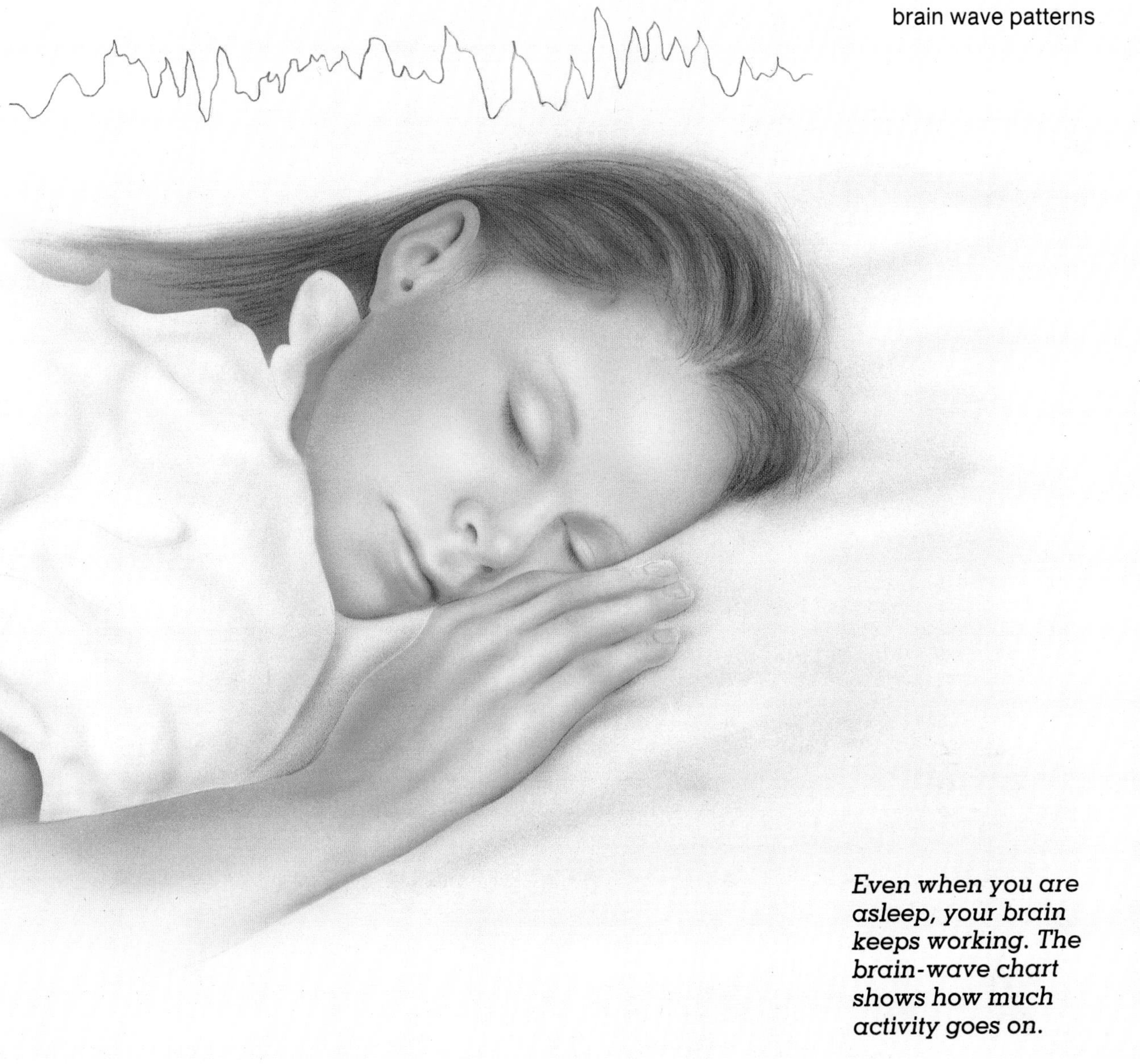

brain wave patterns

Even when you are asleep, your brain keeps working. The brain-wave chart shows how much activity goes on.

Why do we sleep? What goes on during sleep? Many thousands of people have volunteered to help scientists find the answers to these questions. In sleep laboratories, measuring machines show that the brain seems to be resting part of the night. But at other times the sleeping brain is hard at work. The chemical that tells your body to grow is at work mostly during the night. So you wake up a little taller. But when you have reached your full height, that particular body clock shuts itself off.

Dozens of body rhythms begin and end on a regular schedule. And yet all your body clocks usually tick together and in harmony. Most of the time you feel good.

Cells and Tissues

A cell is a blob of living material, so small that you need a microscope to see it. By the time you are grown, you will be made of about 100 trillion cells!

Scientists often say that your cells are the tiny building blocks of your body. Of course, cells aren't at all like blocks. Each one takes in food, breathes, gets rid of waste, and does work.

Constant movement goes on inside a cell. How, for instance, does a cell get rid of waste? The little white circle called a vacuole has that job. It is really a hollow space that can move around inside the cell. When it meets some waste, the vacuole draws itself around the useless material. Then it carries the load to the edge of the cell, where it opens up and dumps the cell's garbage. What moves the vacuole? Scientists know that the moving job is done by little hollow tubes called filaments, but they are not certain how the tubes work.

The parts of a cell are like the members of a community, each one doing a job.

The nucleus is like the president of the group. It directs the other parts. The little dark threads in it were a great puzzle for a long time. Scientists have now solved the puzzle. You'll find the answer on page 68.

The mitochondria change food into energy. (A single one of these is called a mitochondrion.)

Ribosomes take certain substances and turn them into another substance called protein, which the cell uses in several ways.

Your body is made up of trillions of cells. This diagram shows some of a cell's parts. ▶

A Basic Cell

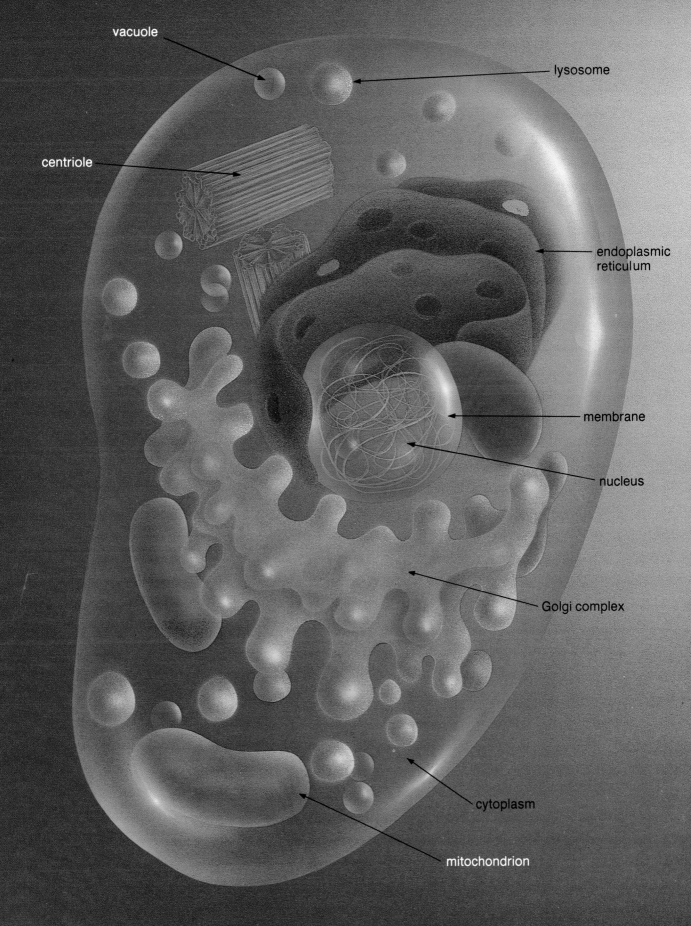

vacuole

lysosome

centriole

endoplasmic reticulum

membrane

nucleus

Golgi complex

cytoplasm

mitochondrion

Lysosomes use some of the protein produced by ribosomes. The main job of the lysosomes is digesting things that aren't needed in the cell. Lysosomes can even digest the cell that is their home. If the cell dies, lysosomes can change it into new material to be used elsewhere in the body.

The Golgi complex is made up of odd-shaped little bags. They are hard to see even with a microscope. They are named for Camillo Golgi, who discovered the complex when he was studying an owl's brain cells. At first, scientists disagreed about the job of the Golgi complex. They now think that the complex is a kind of warehouse where material is packaged for other parts of the cell to use.

Centrioles help out when cells grow and multiply.

The membrane forms the cell's protective coat. It is flexible and thin, so chemicals can pass through it, in and out.

You were born with a complete set of muscle cells. As you grew, these cells got bigger. Other kinds of cells in your body grow differently. Instead of growing larger, they increase in number. First, the nucleus of such cells begins to break up. Then equal parts of the nucleus move to opposite ends of the cell. Next the cell stretches, and a new nucleus forms at each end. Finally the two halves of the cell separate, forming two new cells.

What Kind of Cell Is It?

Whole groups of similar cells working together make up the tissues in your body. Here are a few of the different kinds of cells:

Muscle cells, which are long and thin, are bundled together in muscle tissue.

Nerve cells form the tissue of your brain and nerves.

Special cells make connective tissue. One kind of connective tissue supports and holds your insides in place. Another kind forms tendons and ligaments. The gristly tendons join your muscles to each other or to bone. Ligaments connect bones together.

Cartilage, a tough tissue, is formed by cells that produce both stringy fibers and a glue to hold the fibers together. The tip of your nose is made of cartilage.

Bone cells are soft when they are young. But, gradually, minerals collect around them and give them hard outside coats.

Skin cells, called epithelial cells, form tissues that protect your body in two ways. Epithelial cells on the outside of your body form a tough coat that protects your insides. Soft epithelial cells line your nose and lungs and some other body parts. They produce mucus to keep tissues moist. They also manufacture many different chemicals that digest food and do hundreds of other jobs inside your body.

Cells that are in different parts of your body have different shapes, sizes, and jobs to do. ▶

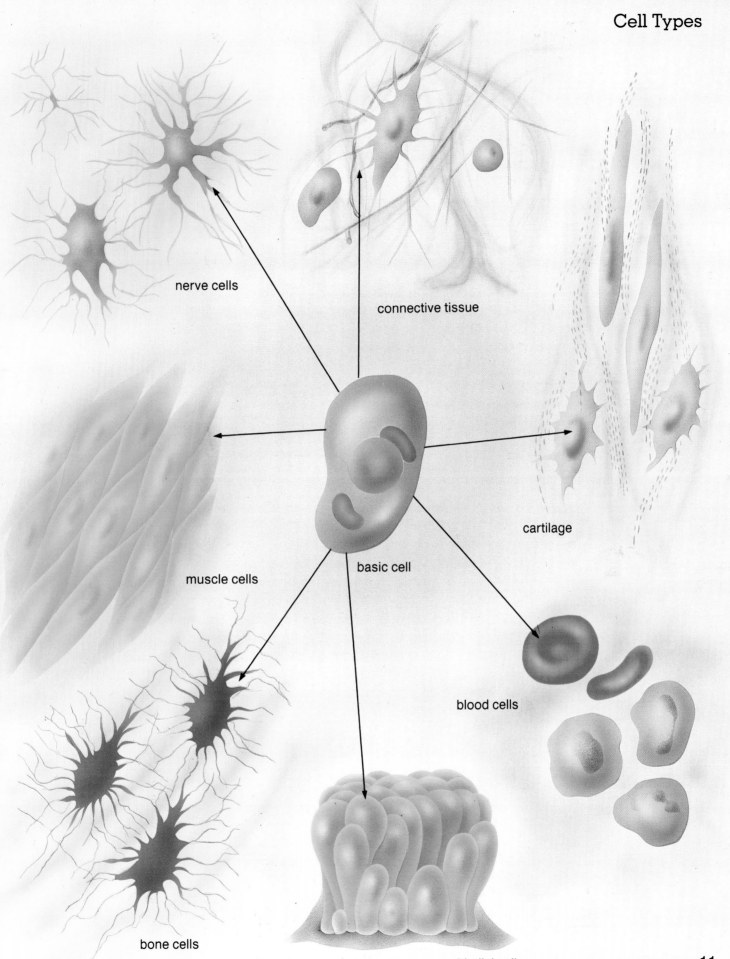

nerve cells

connective tissue

cartilage

muscle cells

basic cell

blood cells

bone cells

epithelial cells

Skin

As you grow, your skin has to cover more and more territory. Does it just keep stretching? For a long time people thought so. But at last scientists figured out what the skin is really like.

Your skin is made of three main layers. The inside layer, called the dermis, is the thickest. Next comes a layer of soft, plump, almost square cells. On top of that middle layer is a sheet of thin material something like kitchen plastic wrap. The middle and top layers are called the epidermis. This is where some fascinating things go on.

For a while the cells in the middle layer do nothing unusual. Then each cell grows slightly bigger and divides into two smaller cells. These grow to full size, and then they divide, making four cells. These divide into eight, then sixteen, and so on.

As the cells multiply, some of them are pushed outward. Their shape changes. They grow flatter and begin to die. What makes them die? As a cell moves toward the surface, tiny fibers of material called keratin grow inside it and begin to kill it. Finally, the dead cells overlap each other and cling together tightly in a tough, almost waterproof film. This is the top layer of the epidermis that covers the whole outside of your body.

It takes almost two months for a cell to be pushed all the way to the surface. Cells beneath it keep moving up, forcing it and many others all the way out—until at last little bunches of dead cells curl up into loose flakes. So many skin flakes leave your body every day that they can actually be seen when a shaft of light comes into a room.

Epithelial cells make up three layers of your skin.
Hair grows out of follicles in the bottom layer. ▶

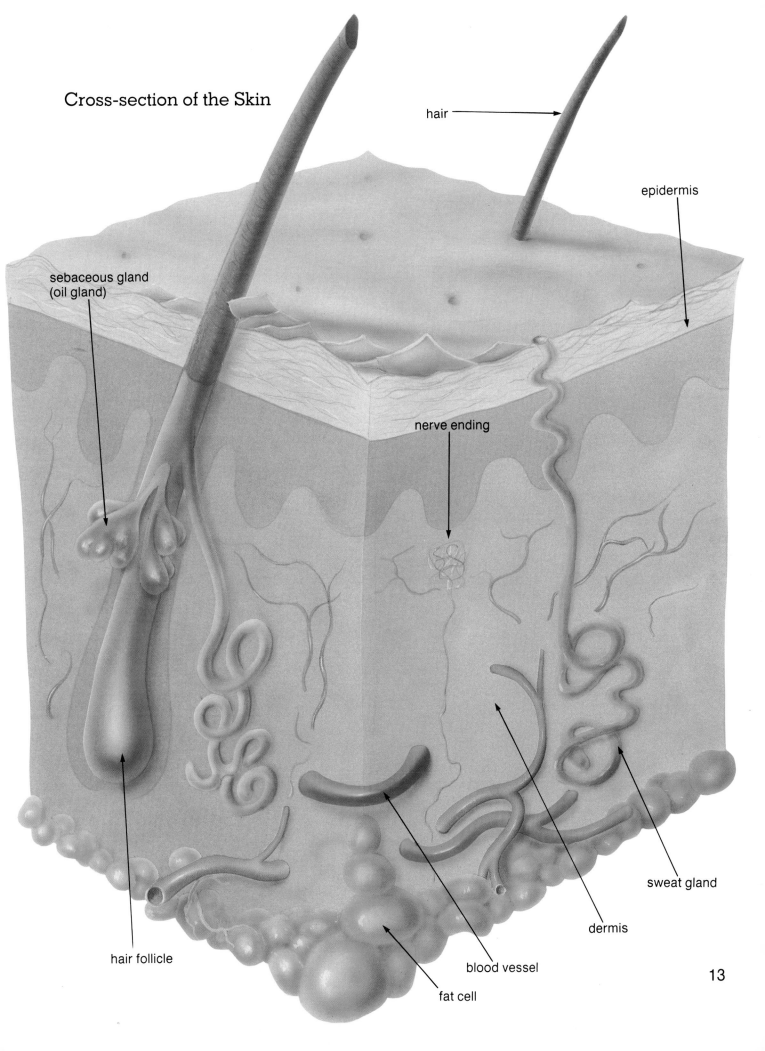

Cross-section of the Skin

hair

epidermis

sebaceous gland
(oil gland)

nerve ending

sweat gland

dermis

hair follicle

blood vessel

fat cell

13

The specks that we call dust floating in the air are mostly flakes of skin cells! Every hour you shed about one million dead skin cells. At the end of a month, you will have an almost completely new epidermis.

The new cells don't form at a steady rate. Around midnight one of your body clocks gives a signal for increased production. From then until about 4 o'clock in the morning, skin cells divide more quickly than at any other time of day. So, if you take a bath in the morning, the ring in your tub consists of more dead skin cells than it does if you take a bath at night.

Skin cells also form the lining of your nose, mouth, and throat and continue down through your lungs, stomach, and intestines. The skin cells in your tongue multiply very fast at night. Look at your tongue in the mirror just before you go to bed. It will be mostly pink with some white down the middle. In the morning, before brushing your teeth, look again. You will see more of a white coat than the night before. With your fingernail gently scrape the top of your tongue, and a bit of thick white stuff called mucus will come off. In it are thousands of dead skin cells that were shed during the night.

Your Skin at Work

One scientist calls the skin a "miracle wrap," because it does so many wonderful things.

By making new cells all the time, your skin can mend itself every time you get a scrape or cut. Special cells in your skin protect you against sunburn. When a lot of sunlight hits them, these cells produce a brownish substance called melanin. Gradually the melanin creeps into other cells and gives them a darker color. The dark cells keep harmful rays of sunlight from burning the sensitive cells underneath.

Your "miracle wrap" helps keep your whole body from getting too hot. Millions of little air conditioners called sweat glands are built into the dermis. These coils of cells produce sweat—a mixture of water and chemicals. When sweat reaches the top layer of skin, it evaporates and carries away heat. An adult's sweat glands produce about two or three cups of water on an ordinary warm day. But in very hot weather the glands really go into action. Exercise makes them work harder, too. During exercise, they can produce as much as ten cups of sweat an hour, provided the person drinks enough water!

Where does all that water come from? The glands draw some of it out of tiny blood vessels nearby in the dermis. The rest comes from lymph, a liquid that constantly bathes the body's cells.

14

Your skin gives you information about what is going on in the outside world. The clear covering at the front of each eye—the cornea—is a special kind of skin that lets in light, so you can see.

Scattered all through the dermis are the tips of nerves that send messages to the brain. Some of the messages tell you that you are cold, or warn you to stand back from a hot stove. Others tell you when something hurts. And still other messages let you know about somebody's soft, comforting touch when you feel sad.

Your skin keeps your delicate inside parts from drying out. It also keeps germs from getting in. And there are plenty of germs ready and waiting to get in. You have more bacteria and other tiny living things called yeasts on your skin than there are people on Earth! They are so tiny that a dozen or more of them could roost on the point of a pin. Their food is the dead cells that come off in flakes from the outside layer of skin. Germs multiply very, very fast. But most of them live only about eighty minutes.

Luckily, most of the germs that live on your skin don't cause you any problems. They don't make you sick. But just in case a harmful one shows up, your skin has a thin film of chemicals that control some germs. Some people even have certain bacteria on their skin that produce a substance called an antibiotic. It actually kills harmful bacteria and keeps cuts from getting infected.

No wonder skin is called a "miracle wrap."

It's a fact that . . .

• People with the darkest skin have the most melanin in their cells. A mixture of melanin and other coloring substances, called pigments, produces different colors in people's skins. When a person gets tanned, the sun's rays cause more melanin to be produced in the melanin cells. Dark-skinned people can get sunburned just as light-skinned people can.

• People without pigment in their cells are called albinos. They usually have white skin, white hair, and pink eyes.

• The ridges in the thick skin on your fingertips are called papillae. The ridges form patterns that make your fingerprints different from everyone else's. That's why fingerprints are often used to identify people.

Digestive System

One day, about 160 years ago, a shotgun went off accidentally at a trading post, close to the border between Canada and the United States. The blast tore a hole in the side of eighteen-year-old Alexis St. Martin, but it did not kill him. The wound healed, but in a strange way. It left an opening right through Alexis's skin and into his stomach.

A flap of the stomach wall kept food from spilling out through the hole. But by pushing the flap aside, Dr. William Beaumont, who took care of Alexis, was able to find out what goes on in a human stomach when food is being digested.

Alexis agreed to let Dr. Beaumont perform some tests. The doctor saw how food is squashed and broken up in the stomach. He saw and tested the chemical juices produced in the stomach. He measured how long it took food to be digested. Altogether, Dr. Beaumont made 238 experiments. These experiments weren't painful, but Alexis found them very boring. One day he got so tired of the whole thing that he went away and never came back.

Scientists and doctors, such as Dr. Beaumont, continued their experiments. Since Dr. Beaumont's time, they have learned much about digestion.

Your teeth cut, crumble, mash, and shred food. But no matter how long you chew, you can't grind the food into bits small enough for the cells of your body to use. Your digestive system makes the little bits smaller.

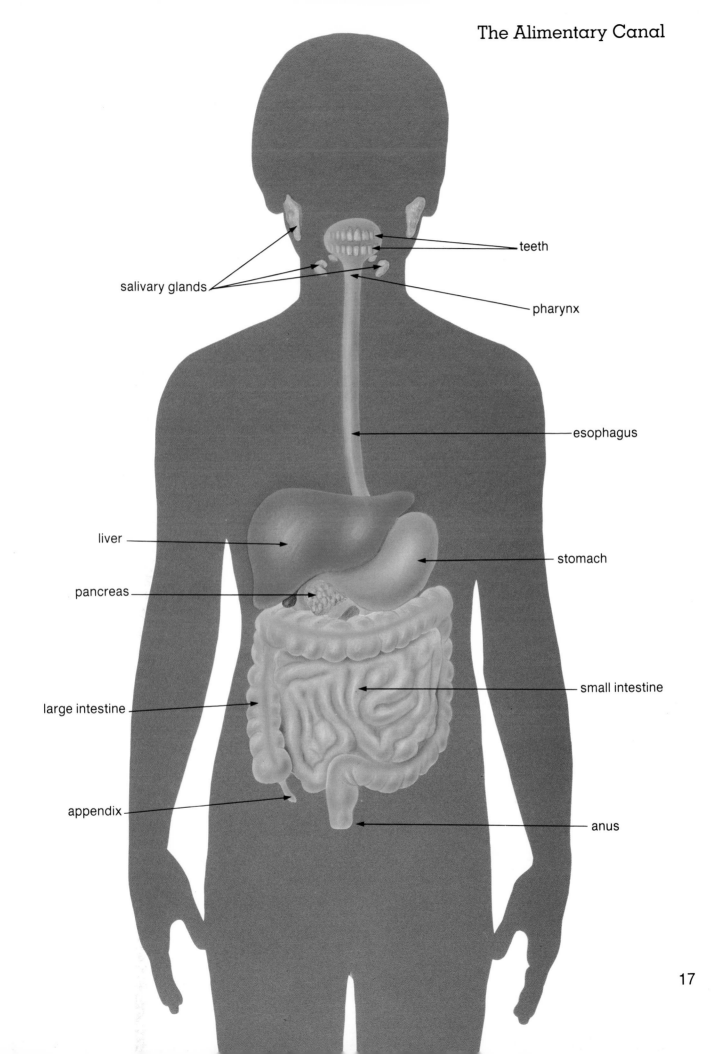

teeth

salivary glands

pharynx

esophagus

liver

stomach

pancreas

small intestine

large intestine

appendix

anus

The Enzymes

As you chew, your tongue and cheek muscles squeeze and mix food with saliva. Just thinking about a delicious sandwich and looking at it on your plate will bring saliva into your mouth. The liquid in saliva moistens the food and makes it easy to swallow. Saliva also contains tiny globe-shaped molecules called enzymes, which start the process of digestion.

To see how an enzyme works, imagine that each tiny molecule has a notched place on top, like the notches in a door key. When an enzyme bumps into a particle of food, such as starch in bread, it fits its key into a matching lock on that bit of starch. Then it gives a sharp twist. And the starch particle breaks apart. It becomes two smaller bits, or molecules, of two different substances that the body can use.

Now the enzyme darts off to catch another starch particle. It works so fast that you couldn't possibly watch each action. A single enzyme can break up several million particles in a minute!

Scientists know that there are at least a thousand different kinds of enzymes at work in your body. Some break up starches and sugars. Some break up the protein in cheese and meat. Others work on butter and other fats. Each kind of enzyme has its own key that fits into a particular lock, so that it can do its special job.

This is how scientists think some enzymes work.

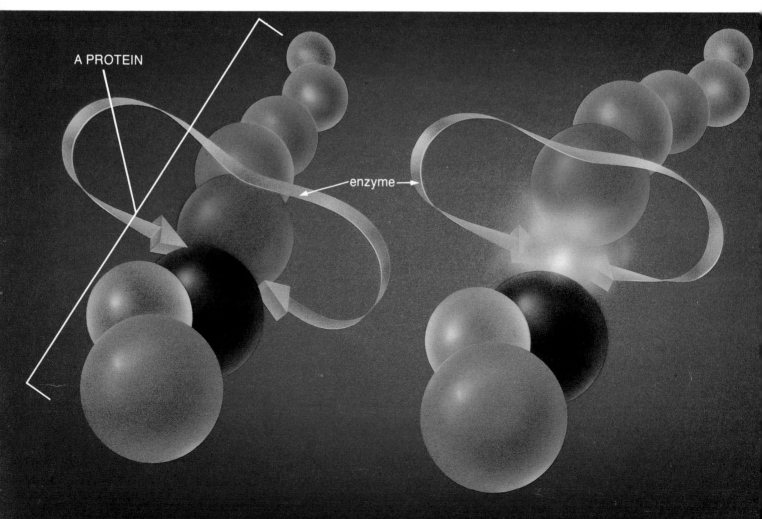

A PROTEIN

←enzyme→

The Esophagus

When you swallow, the bits of a cheese sandwich don't just fall down into your stomach. They leave your mouth and slide into a tube called the esophagus. The muscles in the esophagus squeeze and then relax, in a wave motion, shoving food along. At the top of the stomach, a little gate called a sphincter opens and lets food come in. Then it closes, which keeps the food from spilling out again.

But, when you feel as if you want to vomit, something different happens. To get rid of what is in your sick-feeling stomach, muscles squeeze and push. The sphincter automatically opens and you throw up. Vomiting is one of the body's ways of protecting itself. Usually it makes you feel better.

In the Stomach

Before Dr. Beaumont tested Alexis St. Martin, most people thought that the stomach was just a heavy-duty mixer that squashed food into little pieces. Your stomach does have three bands of strong muscles that churn and squeeze and help to break up bits of food. But Dr. Beaumont found something else. A strong acid produced in the stomach dissolved meat and some other foods. Of course, he couldn't put a microscope inside Alexis's stomach to watch everything that went on. So he missed some amazing things.

Your stomach is lined with epithelial cells. Some of these cells produce a sticky substance called mucus, which coats the whole inside of your stomach. The mucus protects the stomach lining from the acid that pours from groups of cells called glands.

Other glands in the stomach produce millions of enzymes that break up certain food particles. Together, the enzymes and acid are very powerful. They can actually digest the stomach's own lining if it isn't covered with mucus. Altogether about twenty-five million glands squirt the juices into the stomach. At the same time a lot of water seeps in through the walls of blood vessels.

The Small Intestine

Digestion has started, but there are more steps to the job. After your stomach has been squeezing and churning for a while, it begins passing the work on to the next section of your digestive system. From time to time a gate—a sphincter—at the bottom of the stomach lets some liquid flow out into a tube, the small intestine.

Your small intestine is about twenty feet long. It winds back and forth to fit into the lower part of your body, your abdomen. It needs to be so long because it must do so many things in order to keep you well nourished and healthy.

The Stomach and Small Intestine

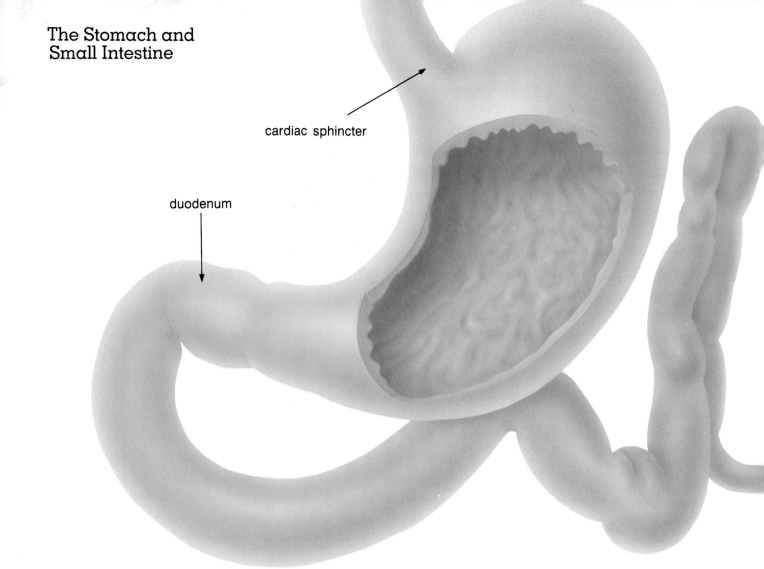

cardiac sphincter

duodenum

Your cardiac sphincter opens to let food into your stomach from your esophagus. The three layers of muscles in the wall of your stomach churn the food and mix it with juices that help to digest it. The pyloric sphincter opens to let food move along into the duodenum.

Food is scarcely out of your stomach before it gets a bath of two juices that pour from a hole in the intestine wall. These juices, which come from the pancreas and the liver, combine with the stomach acid and make it less likely to hurt cells that it might touch. Enzymes in the juices chop up fat molecules that are too big to do your cells any good. Now the fat part of your cheese sandwich becomes more useful. Enzymes and juices also pour out of millions of little groups of cells in the intestine wall. They go to work on the protein in cheese and bread. Still other enzymes break up starches and sugars that are left in any vegetables and fruit you ate.

Full of nourishment, this wonderful soup flows slowly through the small intestine. It goes around bends, even uphill once in a while. What keeps it moving? The intestine squeezes and relaxes, somewhat the way the esophagus does. But movement is helped by tiny waving fingerlike things called villi. Millions and millions of villi line the intestine walls. Each one contains three tubes—two full of blood and one vessel full of a colorless liquid called lymph.

The molecules of starch, sugar, and protein float among the villi. Then suddenly, one after another, they disappear into the blood vessels together with minerals and some of the vitamins in your food.

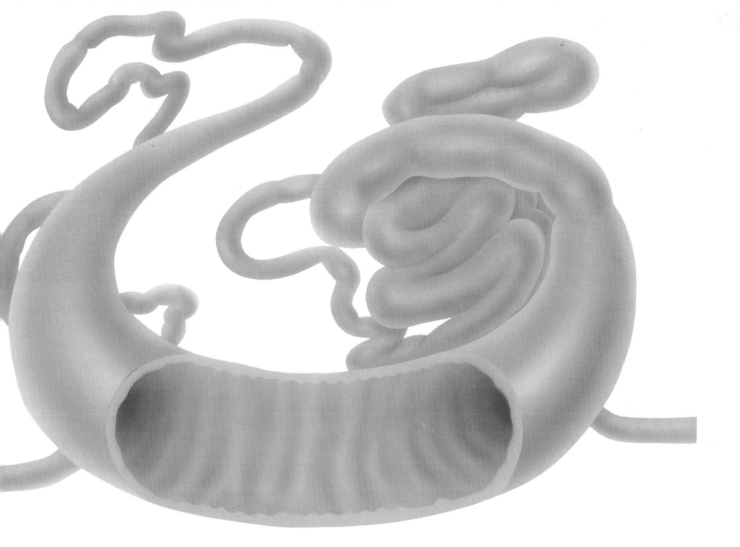

Blood now carries them along on the next part of their journey to nourish your body's cells.

Other vitamins and molecules of fat seem almost to be sucked into the lymph vessels in the villi. We'll catch up with them later on.

The Large Intestine

You may think that by now everything you had for lunch is used up. But there are always some leftovers. They move along, out of the small intestine into a pouch called the cecum at the beginning of a bigger, fatter tube called the large intestine.

Dangling from the cecum is small tube that looks a little like a worm. Scientists named this small tube the *vermiform appendix.* That means "an extra part in the shape of a worm." In humans, the appendix seems to be an unnecessary body part. Sometimes the appendix gets irritated and sore. Scientists don't know why this happens to some people and not to others. When doctors remove the appendix, the patient gets along fine without it.

From the cecum, the thick liquid of undigested food is pushed onward. Suppose you had a piece of celery or an apple for lunch.

The Large Intestine

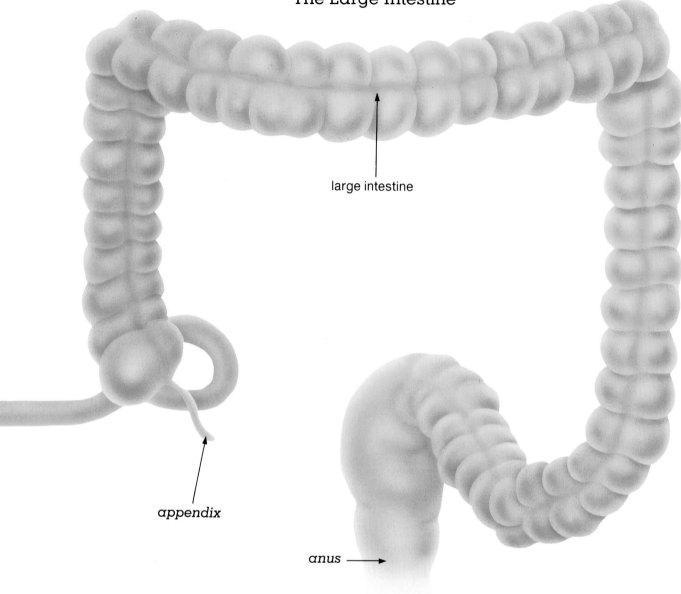

large intestine

appendix

anus →

Celery and apples contain little strings called fiber. So does bread made of whole wheat. The fiber is not digested in the small intestine.

However, bacteria that live in your large intestine are able to use some of these leftovers. They digest some fiber and other substances and turn them into food for themselves. They also turn some of the food material into vitamin K. Your body then uses this vitamin to make other substances that stop the blood flow when you cut yourself. At the same time the bacteria produce waste materials of their own. One of them is gas.

A great deal of gas develops in the intestine when bacteria digest a certain kind of sugar in beans. Pressure from a lot of the gas may sometimes cause a sharp pain. (The gas doesn't smell very good, either.) Can you guess why airplane pilots in World War II, during the 1940s, were forbidden to eat beans? In an airplane high above the earth, the outside air pressure on the body decreases, so gas inside the body can expand and press harder. Pain from the extra pressure might have surprised a pilot into losing control of the plane.

Vast numbers of bacteria live and grow, multiply and die as the last remains of food move through the large intestine. Finally a mass of bacteria and waste reaches the last part of the intestine, called the rectum. In the meantime, much of the water that came from your blood into the stomach and small intestine has been absorbed back into the vessels that line the large intestine wall. Now all that is left is a little bit of undigested material and a very large quantity of dead bacteria. This waste is called feces, and the body gets rid of it through an opening called the anus.

The Liver, Pancreas, and Spleen

Though the liver and pancreas aren't strictly part of your digestive system, they do help change food so that your hundred trillion cells can use it. The pancreas makes a substance called insulin,

---

It's a fact that . . .

• Your body needs vitamins C and B_1, as well as 11 other vitamins in order to stay healthy. How do vitamins help you? They aid in growth. They are important to the health of bones, teeth, skin, and red blood cells. Vitamins also help the blood to clot so that wounds can heal.

• Some information about vitamins has been discovered in unusual ways. In the 1500s, for example, French explorers in Canada found that the Indians there did not suffer from the disease scurvy. Many French sailors did have scurvy, which made their gums sore, loosened their teeth, made their joints ache, and made them lose their appetites. The explorers observed that the Indians drank a tea made from the leaves of an evergreen tree. After the French sailors drank the same tea, their scurvy disappeared! What was the secret medicine found in evergreen leaves? It is a chemical named ascorbic acid, which is now known as vitamin C. Fruits and other vegetables also produce vitamin C, which is why they are necessary parts of a healthy person's diet.

• To be healthy, you must eat foods that supply you with minerals as well as vitamins. If you weigh 80 pounds, about 3 pounds of your weight are minerals such as calcium and iron. For strong bones you need calcium and iron and only tiny amounts of other minerals. Minerals come from fruits, vegetables, meat, and fish. Foods produced by animals, such as milk and eggs, also contain minerals and vitamins.

The Liver, Pancreas, and Spleen

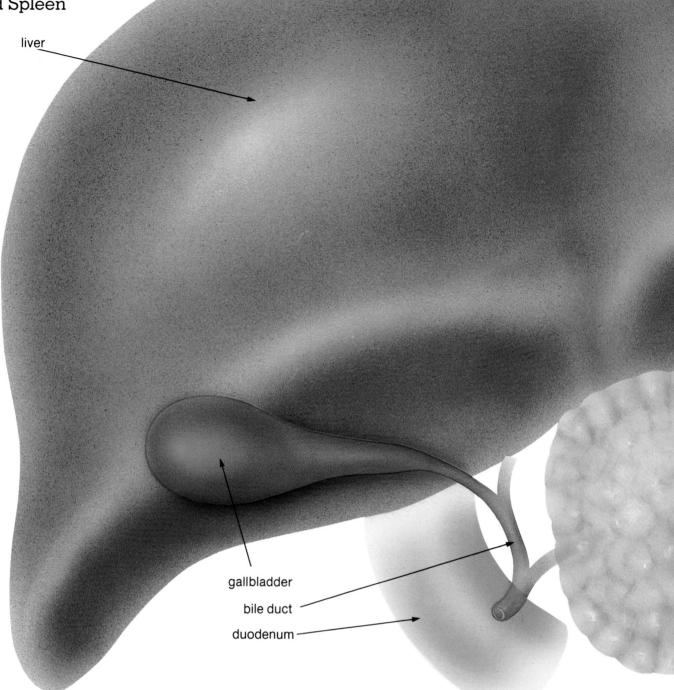

liver

gallbladder

bile duct

duodenum

which controls the amount of sugar that enters the cells. The liver makes a greenish liquid called bile, which helps digest food after it leaves the stomach. Bile is stored in a pouch called the gallbladder. Every day at least a cupful of liquid from the pancreas pours out of a tube that joins another tube carrying the bile. Together, these juices flow through a hole into the small intestine. This is the place, just after food leaves the stomach, where the final steps of digestion begin.

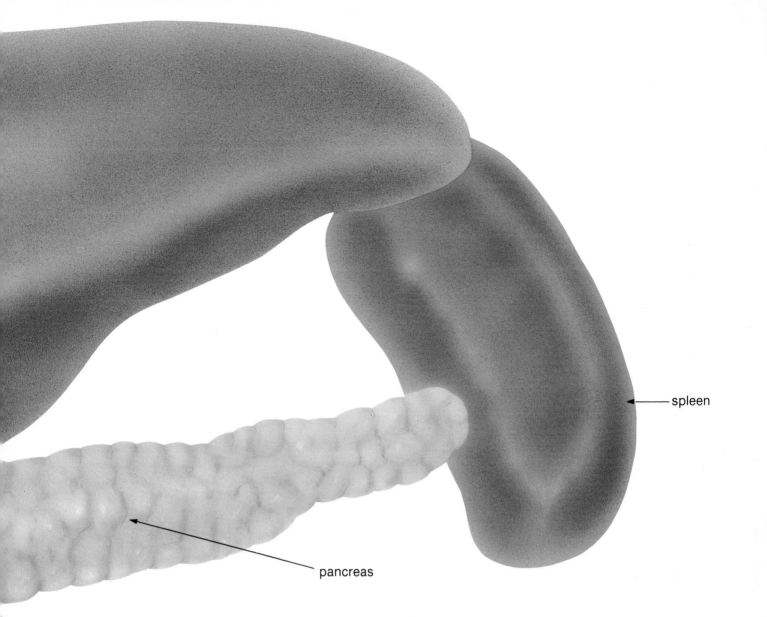

spleen

pancreas

Making bile is only one of the liver's jobs. It does more than seventy others. Inside the liver are thousands of little bunches of cells called lobules. Blood brings food and vitamins to each lobule, which can either store the food and vitamins for future use or send them along to feed your cells. If your body needs extra sugar, the liver can change protein into sugar. No one knew this until a scientist discovered that there is always sugar in the livers of animals who eat only meat.

Here are just a few of the other things the liver does: It manufactures certain chemicals that help to make blood clot in a cut or wound. It destroys red blood cells when they are worn out. It even gets rid of certain poisons that might harm the body.

The spleen helps the liver get rid of worn-out red blood cells. It also acts as a reservoir for blood. If a wound bleeds a lot, the spleen releases its emergency supply of blood into the blood stream.

The liver produces bile that is stored in the gallbladder. Bile helps to digest fats. Juices from the pancreas also help with digestion. The spleen stores an emergency supply of blood.

Circulatory System

For a long time doctors have known that they can tell a healthy heart by the sounds it makes as it beats. In your great-grandparents' day, the doctor just put an ear on a patient's chest or back and listened. That usually worked fairly well. But, one day, there was a patient who was so fat that her doctor couldn't hear a thing. Then he remembered a game that children played on a seesaw in the park. One child would put an ear next to the board at one end of the seesaw. Another child, at the other end, would scratch the board with a pin. The scratching caused tiny vibrations in the wood, and the sound could be heard all the way at the other end of the seesaw.

The moment the doctor remembered this, he made an invention. He rolled a piece of stiff writing paper into a tube and set one end tight against the patient's chest. Sure enough, the vibrations in the tube brought the sound of heartbeats to the doctor's ear. That tube was the first stethoscope. Since then, other inventors have changed and improved the instrument, but the idea is the same.

What is a heartbeat, anyway? Day and night, your heart goes ka-thump, ka-thump, all by itself, through your whole life. Your heart is a kind of pump, made of muscle. The muscle squeezes and relaxes, over and over. Each squeeze pushes blood through tubes, or vessels, to every part of your body.

Like a pump in a well, the heart has its own electric motor, called a pacemaker. The pacemaker is a small clump of cells in the right side of the heart. These special cells send out little bursts of electric

26

An adult's body has 60,000 miles of blood vessels. The heart pumps blood through them. ▶

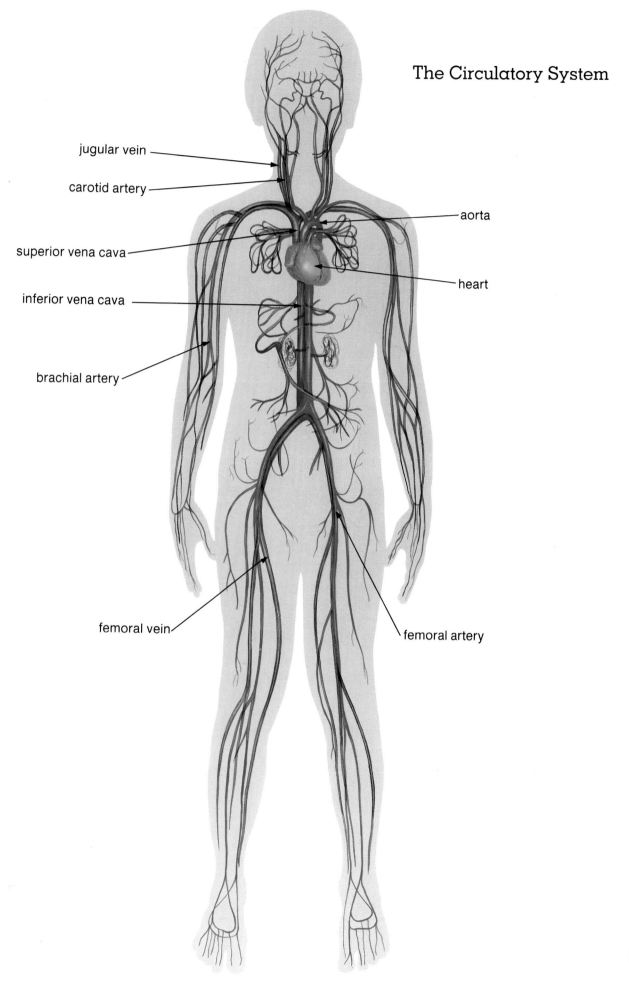

The Circulatory System

jugular vein

carotid artery

aorta

superior vena cava

heart

inferior vena cava

brachial artery

femoral vein

femoral artery

How the Heart Beats

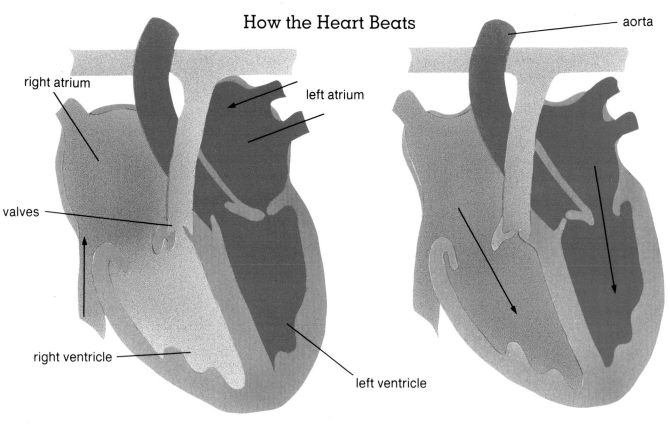

right atrium

left atrium

valves

aorta

right ventricle

left ventricle

1. The atria fill with blood.

2. The atria contract.

current about seventy times a minute. The current signals the heart muscle to contract and squeeze. Between signals the muscle relaxes. Your heart beats more than 100,000 times in a day. It rests for only a fraction of a second after each beat.

Miles of Blood Vessels

The picture on page 27 shows some of the complicated paths of the blood vessels—out of the heart, through the body, and back again to the heart. No picture could show all the paths, because some blood vessels, the capillaries, are so tiny that you need a microscope to see them. It would take an artist years to draw them all. Why? Because there are 60,000 miles of blood vessels in an adult's body. If you could lay all of those tubes, large and small, end to end, they would go around the earth almost 2½ times.

Look carefully at the picture, and you will see that the blood comes into the heart through a vessel called a vein at the top of the right side. This is blood that has traveled up from your feet, and in from your fingers, your skin, and other organs. It has also made its way through the insides of the tiny villi in your intestines and on through your liver, picking up digested food.

The blood now has a load of food it can carry to cells all over the body. But it still has to pick up oxygen, which cells also need. First the

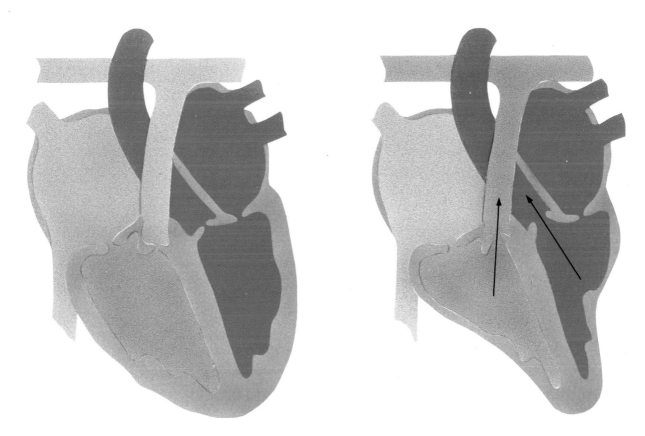

3. Atrial valves close.   *4. Ventricles contract.*

blood goes from a pocket, or chamber, at the top of the right side of the heart, through a valve, into a chamber at the bottom. Then, when the pacemaker signals for a squeeze, the right part of the heart muscle contracts. This pushes blood toward the lungs, where it will get a load of oxygen.

Squeeze, push—about three tablespoonfuls at a time, blood leaves the heart and moves toward the lungs. From the lungs it flows into the top chamber of the *left* side of the heart. Our hearts have four chambers to give the blood an extra push that sends it to all the places that need it. At the signal from the pacemaker, the top left chamber of the heart sends blood into the bottom left chamber. Then the bottom left chamber gives a very strong squeeze that sends the blood on through the arteries.

Your heart really acts like two hearts. Both do their pumping at the same time. But the left side pushes much harder than the right. It makes more noise than the right one, too. So that is the heartbeat that the doctor hears with a stethoscope.

At certain places the walls of arteries also expand and then contract, helping the blood to move along. You can feel the throbbing of this wavelike motion if you press your fingers against a spot on your wrist where an artery is quite near the surface. The throbbing is called your pulse. The pulse is not a heartbeat, but its timing is the same—about seventy throbs a minute.

From an artery, blood goes through smaller vessels called arterioles into still smaller ones, the capillaries. The walls of these tiny vessels are so thin that molecules of food can slip through them. So can oxygen and other things that cells need.

The blood flows on, into more capillaries and finally into the vessels called veins. These have little gates, or valves, that open to let blood through, then close to keep it from sliding back. And so blood comes to the heart again, completing a circular trip. That is why the heart and the blood vessels are called the circulatory system.

Round-Trip on a Red-Cell Raft

A grown person's body has about twenty-four cups of blood. Part of this blood, called plasma, is liquid. It is yellowish and mostly water. The red color of blood comes from red blood cells. Your blood has about twenty trillion of these cells. They are so small that five million of them could fit in a drop the size of the dot on the letter *i*.

One scientist called the red cells "rafts" for carrying oxygen, and they do look a bit like miniature rubber rafts. The oxygen is attached to a red substance called hemoglobin, which gives the cell its color.

Imagine a red cell that has just been manufactured in a tissue called marrow. The new cell pops into the bloodstream and starts its journey toward the lungs to pick up a load of oxygen. Even though it is so tiny, the cell can carry about 265 molecules of hemoglobin. In the lungs, the red-cell "raft" travels through tiny narrow blood vessels, the capillaries. A capillary is only one cell wide. So the red cell must twist and bend, pushed from behind by other red cells that are picking up oxygen. This rough treatment is hard on the cell. But it comes through safely.

A new red cell will spend about four months rafting around and around through blood vessels. Before the cell wears out, it will make about 160,000 trips to and from the heart. About 2½ million red cells die every second. (At the same time 2½ million new ones are created.) The broken, worn-out cells are not wasted. The bloodstream carries them through the liver and spleen, and there they are recycled. Parts of the dead cells soon appear again in new red cells.

Other Blood Cells

Blood also contains white blood cells. They work like detectives. Several kinds wander around the bloodstream, and some can even move against the current in the bloodstream if they need to. These wanderers have the job of protecting you against germs and against any chemicals that don't belong in your body. A lot of white cells wait

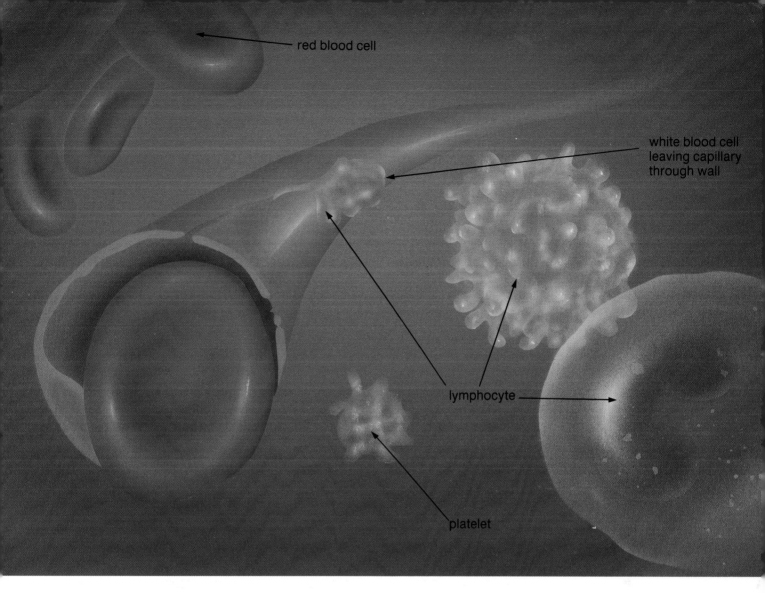

red blood cell

white blood cell leaving capillary through wall

lymphocyte

platelet

in the spleen, ready to pounce on invaders. When a white cell finds some germs, the cell suddenly gets bigger. Then it quickly divides, creating many new cells that all pursue the germs.

Platelets are often called cells, but they are really fragments of other cells. Each platelet contains a chemical that helps your blood to clot if you get a cut. The clot stops the bleeding, and usually it keeps germs out of the wound.

But suppose you cut your finger and some germs do get in. They multiply and cause an infection. Soon your white cells receive signals from certain chemicals that the infection produces. The wandering white cells then slither their jellylike bodies out of capillaries near the cut.

Red cells carry oxygen. White cells protect your body against germs and alien chemicals.

Blood Puzzles

More than 500 years ago, doctors among the Inca Indians of South America knew a great deal about medicine. If an Inca was hurt and lost a lot of blood, a doctor could give the victim a transfusion. In a transfusion, blood from an uninjured person is put through a tube into the injured person's blood vessels.

Long after Inca times, doctors in Europe also tried to perform transfusions. But many of their patients who got blood became even more ill.

Time passed. Doctors tried to figure out why some transfusions didn't work. Then, in the 1800s, Dr. Karl Landsteiner, an American doctor born in Austria, made a discovery. He found that red cells contain two different substances, which he named type A and type B. Dr. Landsteiner's test on patients showed that some had type A

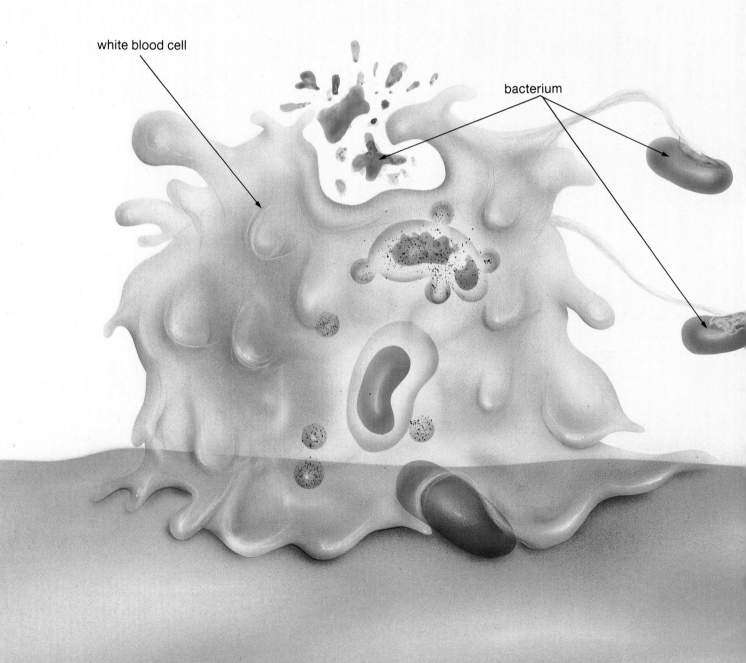

white blood cell

bacterium

substance in their cells and other patients had type B. Some had neither. Dr. Landsteiner named their type O.

Tests showed that type A people could have transfusions of type A blood. Type B people could be given type B blood. Type AB people—those with both substances—could be given A, B, or AB blood. Type O people could only receive type O blood. Yet it is safe to give type O blood to A, B, or AB people.

Why, then, were the Incas successful with blood transfusions? Most Indian people in South America have type O blood. It is possible that, in Inca days, all Indians were type O. So they could safely give and receive blood in transfusions among themselves.

◀ *Some white cells travel around the body ready to attack invaders. When a cell finds a germ or bacterium, it wraps itself around the bacterium and digests it.*

Immune System

Why do people get colds and other diseases? That used to be one of the world's greatest mysteries. Then about one hundred years ago, a scientist, Louis Pasteur, discovered that tiny things called germs make people sick.

Still, no one knew how people got well again or how the body fought germs. Years went by, and then another scientist found part of the answer. Certain white blood cells, he discovered, can track down disease bacteria and destroy them. But another problem was not solved: How does the body deal with another kind of germ—a virus? Scientists solved that problem when they discovered virus-fighters in the body. The scientists named them *antibodies*.

This is how antibodies work: Special white blood cells called lymphocytes wander about in your blood. On the surface of a lymphocyte is a speck of chemical with a shape of its own. This speck is an antibody. Its shape will fit into a certain spot on a foreign substance, such as a virus that doesn't belong in the body. Suppose a lymphocyte senses that a virus invasion has started. The lymphocyte immediately grows and produces new cells called plasma cells. The plasma cells release a flock of antibodies that swim off and fit themselves onto the germs. This makes the germs helpless, and the invasion stops then and there. Finally, white cells of another kind called phagocytes appear and digest the now harmless invaders.

A white cell uses antibodies to attack a virus. ▶

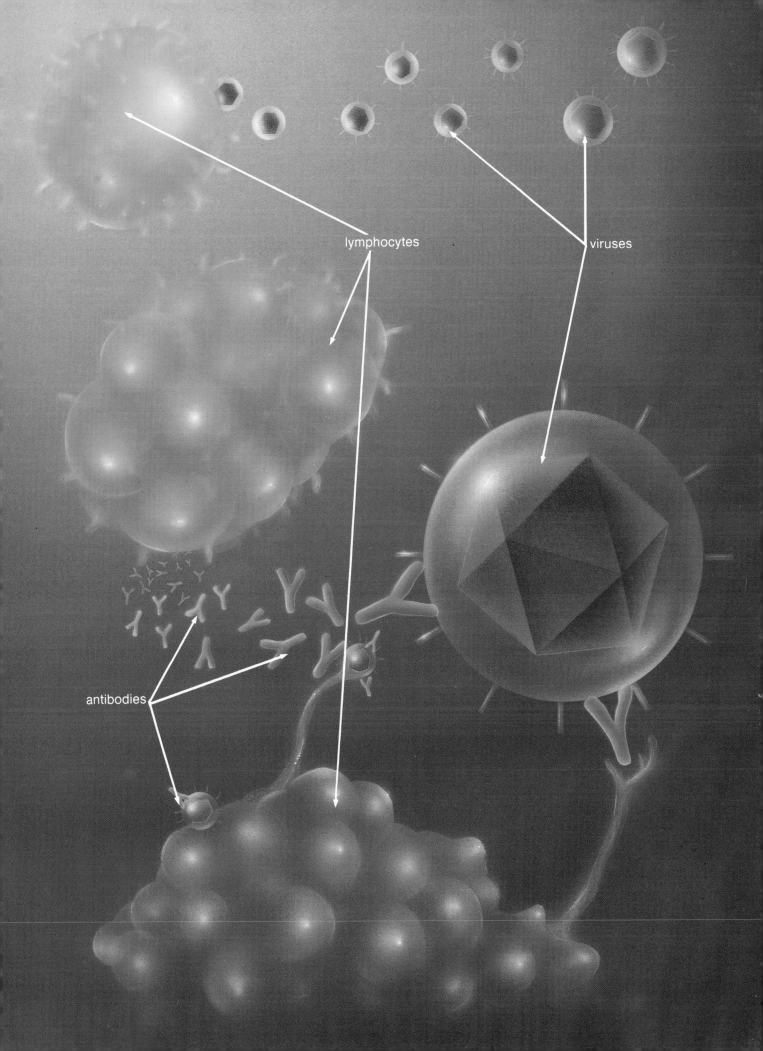

lymphocytes

viruses

antibodies

Viruses and Memory Cells

Sometimes a virus that causes a disease, such as chicken pox, gets a head start on your lymphocytes. At first the antibodies on your lymphocytes can't take care of the germs. But after about two weeks, your antibodies win and you get well. In the meantime, an amazing thing has happened. The invasion leaves some cells in your blood that "remember" this particular virus. If chicken pox virus gets into your body at a later time, these "memory" cells create vast numbers of plasma cells. The plasma cells then release so many antibodies that the invaders don't have a chance. This means you'll never get chicken pox again. You are now immune to the disease. The system that protects you is called the immune system.

Scientists have discovered how to keep you from ever getting certain diseases, such as measles and diphtheria. In a laboratory, the scientists kill or weaken some of the viruses that cause the disease. Then, with a sharp little needle, your doctor injects some of the weak or dead germs into your arm. You don't get sick, but your cells will make antibodies and "memory" cells anyway. Now you will be immune to that disease.

White cells also protect you if certain foreign chemicals get into your body. They can make antibodies against chemicals that were not even invented till after you were born!

Sneeze Makers

Do you have an allergy? Perhaps you sneeze when certain flowers bloom. Pollen from the flowers is the cause. A tiny grain of pollen reaches the inside of your nose and spills out bits of a chemical. The chemical invades your cells, and for some reason your antibodies don't get rid of the invader. Instead, the cells seem to explode. Out comes a substance called histamine that, together with some other chemicals, irritates your nose and makes you sneeze. Scientists aren't sure why this happens. And it is still a mystery why some people have allergies and others don't.

It's a fact that . . .

- Lymph nodes are formed by knobs of tissue in the lymph system.
- Tonsils and adenoids are lymph nodes.
- As lymph flows through the nodes, bacteria and some waste matter are destroyed.

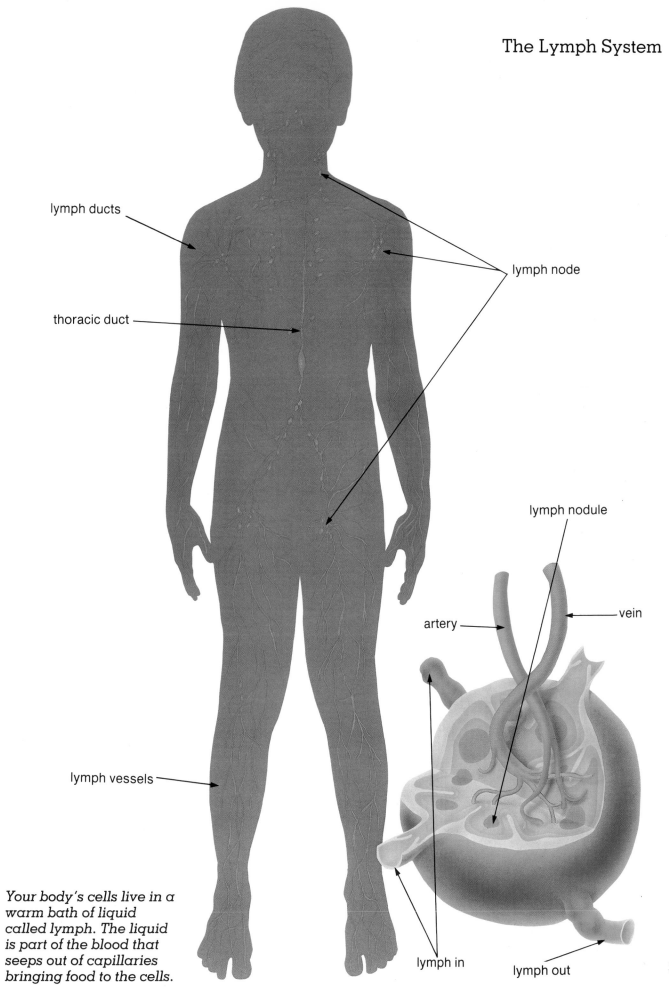

lymph ducts

lymph node

thoracic duct

lymph nodule

vein

artery

lymph vessels

Your body's cells live in a warm bath of liquid called lymph. The liquid is part of the blood that seeps out of capillaries bringing food to the cells.

lymph in

lymph out

37

Respiratory System

About two hundred years ago, nobody knew much about air. Then several men did experiments and discovered that what you breathe is a mixture of gases. One of the gases made wood burn very fast, and the scientist who found this out named the gas "fire air." Another experimenter discovered that mice got very lively when they breathed a lot of that same gas. Scientists, who named the gas oxygen, went on to learn its secrets.

The other gases in the air are important, but oxygen is the one that people and animals must get from the air when they breathe. How do their bodies use the oxygen? The burning wood experiment gave part of the answer. Oxygen combines with certain substances in wood and creates heat when it burns. Oxygen also combines with food and produces heat and energy in the body. You need extra energy when you exercise. So you breathe harder to bring in more oxygen.

Nose on Guard

Another word for breathing is respiration. Your respiratory system begins with your nose. You almost always breathe through your nose, unless you have a cold or have been exercising hard. There are good reasons why you do this. Your nose acts as a guard at the outside gate to your sensitive lungs. First the air travels past some hairs inside the nose. The hairs trap some of the larger dust particles in air and keep them from getting into your lungs. Other bits of dust,

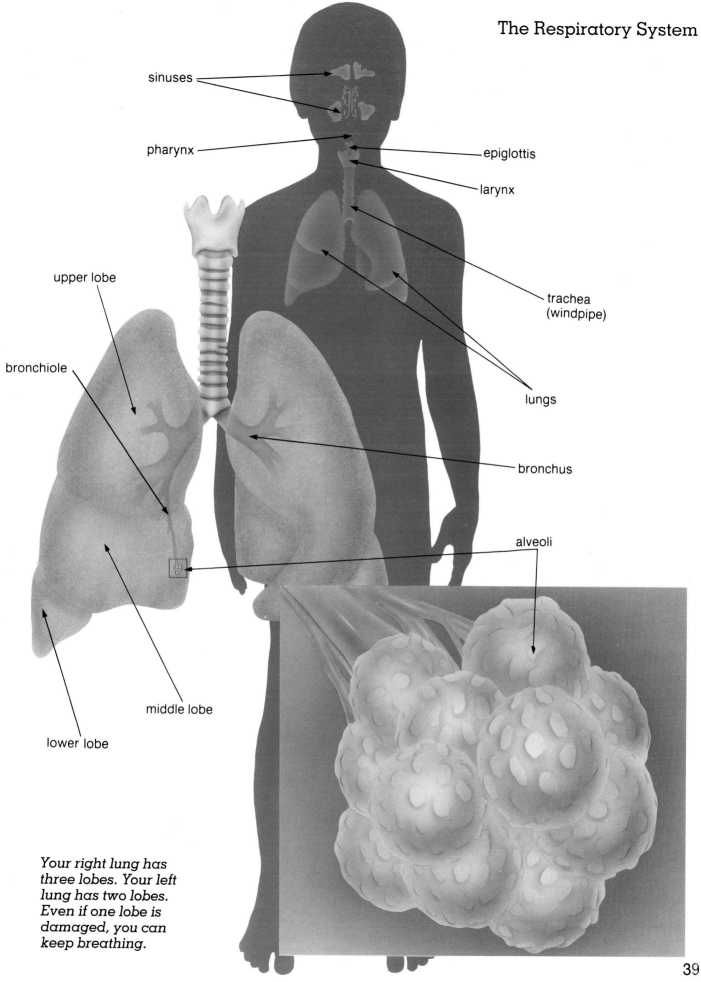

sinuses

pharynx

epiglottis

larynx

trachea (windpipe)

lungs

upper lobe

bronchiole

bronchus

alveoli

middle lobe

lower lobe

Your right lung has three lobes. Your left lung has two lobes. Even if one lobe is damaged, you can keep breathing.

and germs too, get caught in a sticky film called mucus that certain cells in the nose manufacture.

The mucus-making cells also line your throat and windpipe and the tubes that lead down into your lungs. Underneath the mucus the cells are covered with a whole forest of tiny hairlike things called cilia. The cilia sway back and forth, as if a wind is constantly blowing on them. There are so many of them that they push the mucus gently along. Every once in a while you cough or clear your throat and get rid of a sticky glob full of dirt and germs. The cilia don't depend on any nerves or any organ to send them signals. They sway together in rhythm, all by themselves, doing their job.

The CO$_2$ Story

Like you, school children in the 1800s sometimes stood in line outdoors during recess. But they had to do a special exercise. They took deep breaths while their teacher chanted, "In comes the good

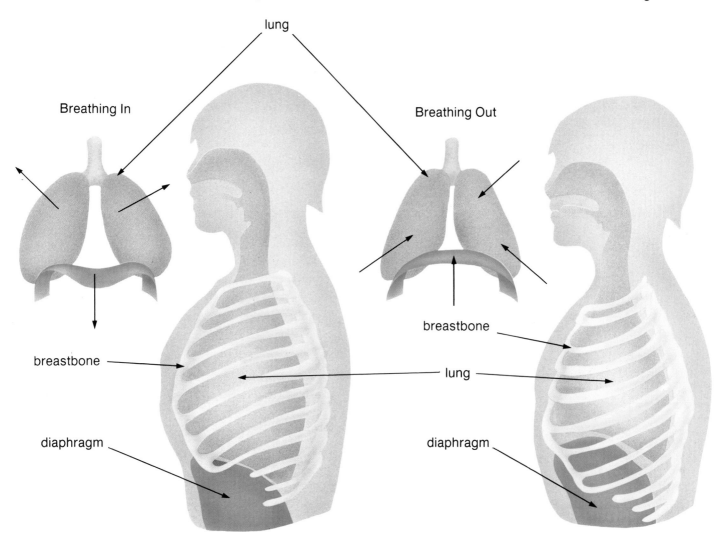

lung

Breathing In

breastbone

diaphragm

Breathing Out

breastbone

lung

diaphragm

air. Out goes the bad air." The "good air" was oxygen. What was called "bad air" was another gas—carbon dioxide, or CO_2.

Is carbon dioxide really bad for you? No. It is as necessary as oxygen, but in a different way. Carbon dioxide is formed when food combines with oxygen in your cells. Your cells can't use it, so molecules of the gas are carried away in the blood. When the carbon dioxide molecules reach your lungs, they pop out into the alveoli, where your breathing gets rid of them.

The amount of carbon dioxide that leaves your body is usually balanced by the oxygen that comes in. But suppose you run a race. Your muscles work hard and use up more oxygen than usual. This puts extra carbon dioxide into your blood. Soon you begin to pant. But you don't actually decide to breathe faster in order to bring in more oxygen. The panting starts automatically, because a patch of brain cells sends a message to your breathing apparatus. This one part of the brain is able to sample your blood as it flows by. When the brain cells detect the extra carbon dioxide, emergency signals go out and you breathe faster and more deeply.

This special breathing control center in the brain works automatically all the time. When it detects the right amount of carbon dioxide in the blood, its signals make you breathe normally—not too slowly, not too fast. Of course, you can decide to breathe faster and more deeply, but another part of the brain sends out the signals for that. You can also decide not to breathe for a while. But you can't hold your breath for very long. The cells in the control center are the bosses. They send out signals that force you to take a breath and bring necessary oxygen into your lungs. And so it isn't oxygen that makes you breathe. It's CO_2!

Air Pump

Your lungs act like a pump, and the pump's motor is a group of muscles driven by the signals from your brain. One big sheet of muscle, called the diaphragm, stretches underneath your lungs, all the way from your breastbone to your backbone. Other pumping muscles are attached to your ribs. When signals tell all of them to tighten up, they get shorter. They pull the ribs up and outward, and the diaphragm becomes flat. This makes the chest cavity bigger, and there is less pressure on the lungs. With more room and less pressure inside, the outside air can rush in.

At the next signal, the muscles relax. The ribs settle back and the diaphragm rises. This creates pressure against the lungs, and air is pushed out.

The diaphragm contracts and relaxes when you breath in and out.

Excretory System

In ancient times people used the word *excrete* when they talked about sifting flour. Scientists have given the name excretory system to the body's method of sifting waste materials out of the blood. (Other wastes—the solid kind—leave through the intestine.) The excretory system begins with the kidneys.

Your kidneys are two bean-shaped organs, each about the size of your fist. You can think of them as two recycling factories, each with a million tiny workers constantly on the job. The scientific name for these workers is nephrons. Each nephron takes waste out of the blood and then puts back into the bloodstream everything that is useful. What happens as the nephrons do their work?

Blood comes rushing into a nephron through a cluster of capillaries. Some of the liquid part of the blood seeps through into the nephron's little tubes. As the liquid flows along, special cells in the tubes begin testing it. (One scientist says they "taste" it!) Automatically, the recycling process begins.

The nephrons test for salt, take some of it out, and send just the right amount back into the blood. They send back the food and most of the vitamins that are floating in the liquid. They test all the chemicals and send back only the ones the body needs.

There is a lot of water in the liquid, and the nephrons figure out exactly how much to send back. For example, if you have been sweating heavily, they send back a lot of the water. The water the nephrons don't send back is collected in tubes that drain out of the kidneys.

The male urethra is longer than the female urethra. This is the only difference between the male and female excretory systems. ▶

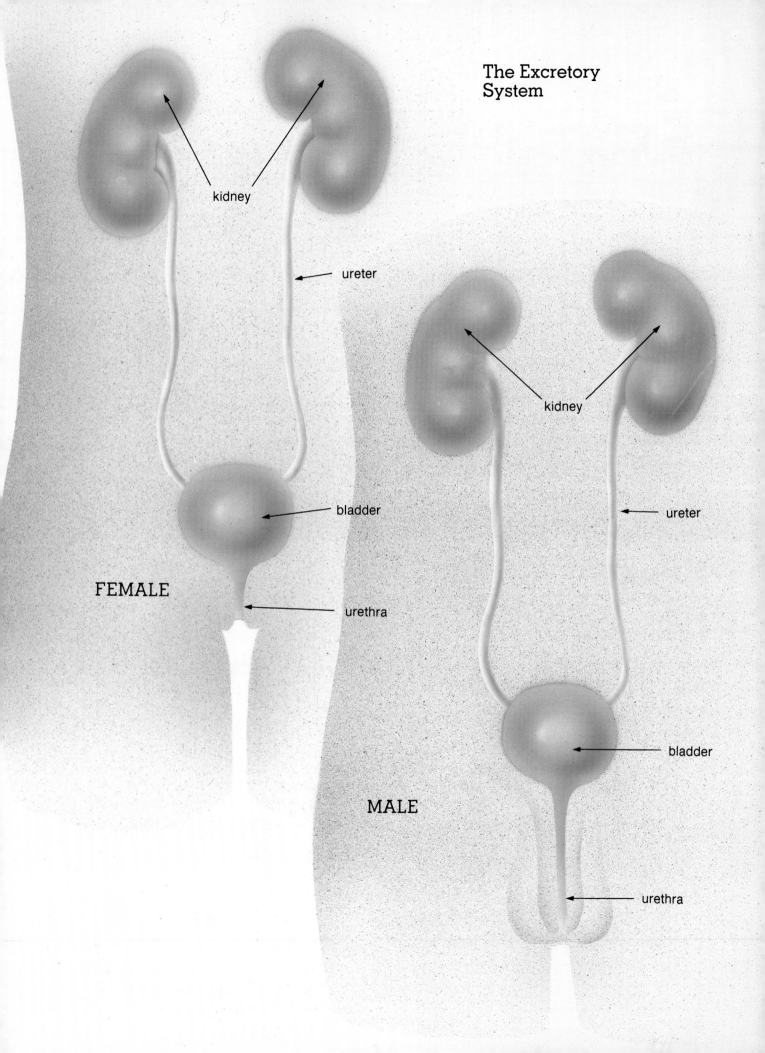

The Excretory System

kidney

ureter

bladder

FEMALE

urethra

kidney

ureter

bladder

MALE

urethra

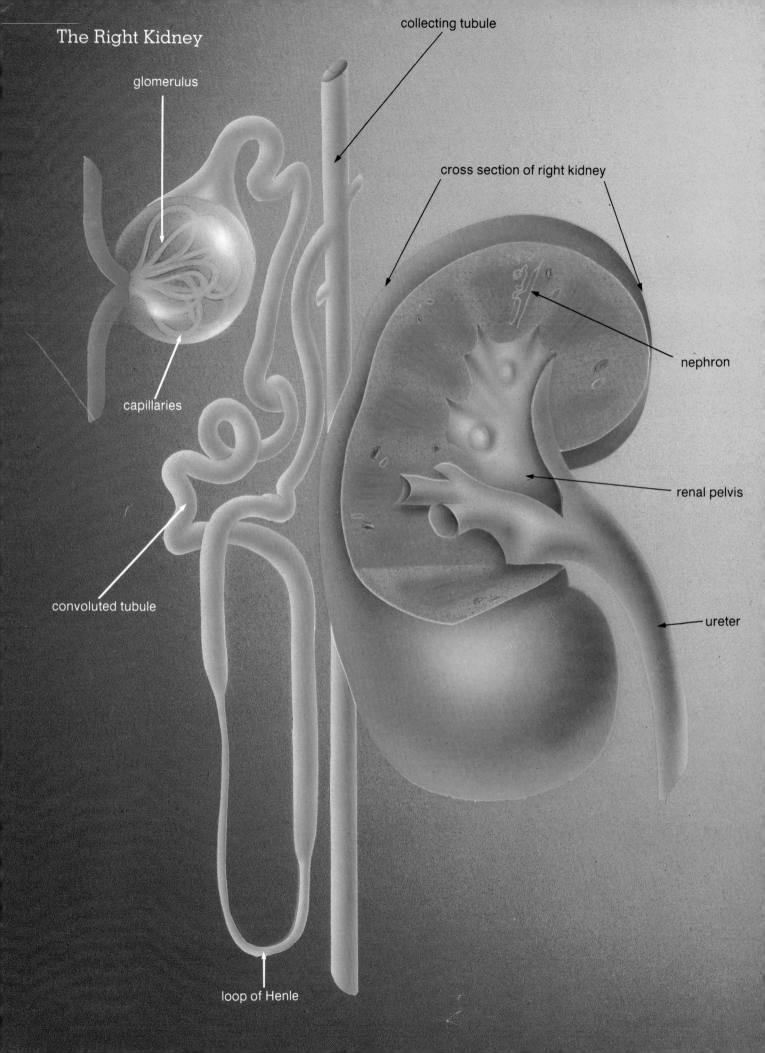

The Right Kidney

collecting tubule

glomerulus

cross section of right kidney

nephron

capillaries

renal pelvis

convoluted tubule

ureter

loop of Henle

The nephrons recognize waste substances that are left over after the body's cells use food. Other wastes come from organs such as the liver. All of these wastes are taken out. When they are mixed with water in the nephrons' tubes, they form what is called urine. So this system is also called the urinary system.

From the kidneys, urine flows down into the bladder, a sac that can expand. When about a cupful of urine has collected, nerves in the bladder carry a message to the brain. At first the brain doesn't pay attention to it. But as more urine collects, much stronger messages go out, and the bladder must be emptied.

The lower tip of the bladder is held closed by a ring-shaped muscle—a sphincter. Most adults can control this muscle even when the bladder contains quite a lot of urine. The sphincter opens when it gets a message from the thinking part of the brain. Babies can't control their sphincter muscle. When a baby's brain gets a message that urine has collected, the muscle relaxes and opens automatically, and the bladder is emptied.

The excretory system operates in a very exact way. It helps to make sure that there is not too much or too little of any substance in your blood. This helps keep you healthy.

It's a fact that . . .

- Working together, the two million nephrons in your kidneys take waste material out of your blood. Because there are so many nephrons, they clean all your blood once every 45 minutes. Some scientists even claim the nephrons do the job in 20 minutes!
- Every day the nephrons send about six cups of urine to the bladder.
- Urine gets its yellow color from leftover chemicals in the bile.

The inside of a kidney looks like this.

Brain and Central Nervous System

Your brain is the headquarters of your nervous system. Nerve cells—neurons—in your brain connect with other neurons in a network that reaches all the organs in your body.

No one knows exactly how many neurons there are in your whole body. Some scientists say there are ten billion. Others say there are seventy-five or even 100 billion. At any rate, most of them are in your brain.

A neuron has three parts. Like other cells, it has a cell body. It also has thin spidery fibers called dendrites at one side of the cell body. At the opposite side of the cell body is a long fiber called an axon, which ends in little branches like fingers. Some axons are wrapped in fatty white material, which makes them look like strings of tiny sausages. Some neurons are short. Others go all the way from the middle of your back to your feet.

Neurons are pathways for electrical signals that travel to and from your brain. A signal from the neuron's cell body zips along the axon to its tips, which almost touch the dendrites of the next neuron. The narrow space between the two neurons is called a synapse. With the help of chemicals in the synapse, the signal leaps across the space to the dendrites of the next neuron. Then it travels through the dendrites to that neuron's cell body.

Billions of neuron cell bodies form a gray mass that makes up the top part of the wrinkled cap in your cerebrum. This mass is called the gray matter. Underneath it, the neurons' axons in their fatty coverings make up the white matter.

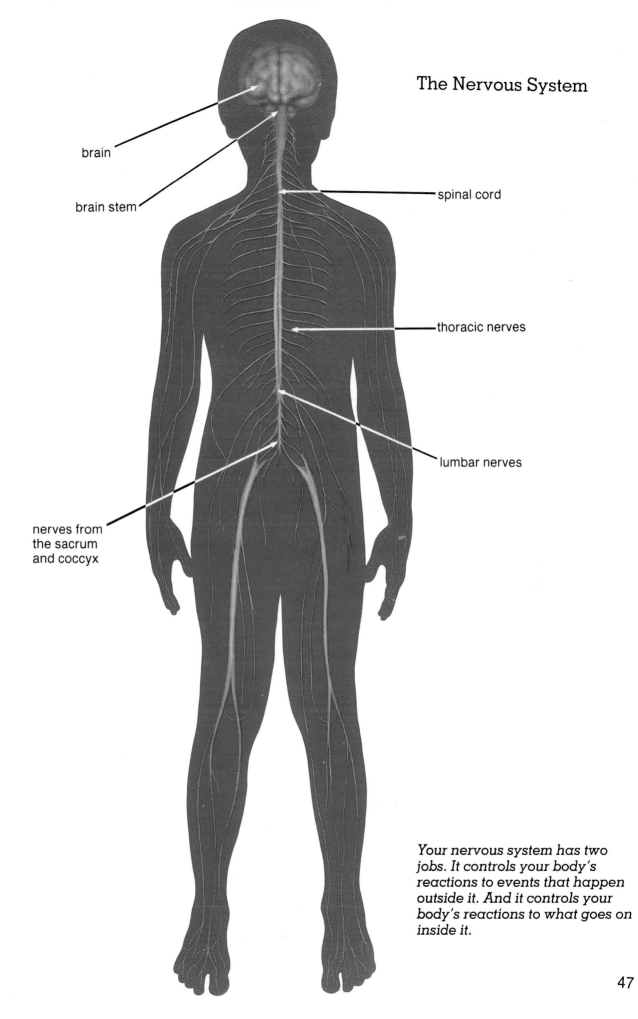

The Nervous System

brain

brain stem

spinal cord

thoracic nerves

lumbar nerves

nerves from
the sacrum
and coccyx

*Your nervous system has two
jobs. It controls your body's
reactions to events that happen
outside it. And it controls your
body's reactions to what goes on
inside it.*

47

Your brain is bigger now than it was when you were a baby, but it hasn't developed any new neurons since then. You were born with all the neurons that you will ever have in your brain. Some of your neurons even disappeared as you grew. Then how did your brain grow? Other brain cells, called glia, did increase in number. Glia means glue, but the glia don't really stick to anything. They support and cushion the neurons. Do the glia also pass along some electrical signals? Scientists are still trying to find out.

The neurons in your brain form a marvelous network, with dendrites from one cell connecting that cell to others. As you grow and learn, you get new connections between neurons. When you began to walk and talk, millions of new pathways formed from one neuron to another. Still more connections formed when you began to have thoughts, learned to read and to use your hands for writing or drawing. Scientists know that somehow all these connections help you to remember things. But it is not known exactly how memory works.

A Cable Down Your Back

Your spinal cord begins at your neck and runs about two-thirds of the way down inside your backbone. The spinal cord is a cable of neurons that connects your brain with your spinal nerves. It allows messages to travel between your brain and the other parts of your body. Some sensory nerves and motor nerves meet in the spinal cord. This is an important arrangement for the relaying of some messages. Suppose you step on a sharp rock with a bare foot. Instantly a message shoots back along a motor nerve. You jerk your foot up even before a pain message reaches your brain. Often, this kind of action, called a reflex action, protects you from harm.

Your brain is always at work, day and night. Scientists know which parts of it give you the ability to speak and do many other things, such as read, write, and draw. But, for a long time, scientists weren't sure what part of your brain makes you dream. Then a wounded soldier helped them learn more about this. The soldier was wounded in a battle less than thirty years ago. A piece of metal stuck in the part of his brain stem called the pons. Doctors couldn't remove the metal. It stayed in the man's brain, even after he got well. From then on he almost never dreamed again. Scientists now think that, during dreams, neurons in the pons may be receiving messages from certain parts of the brain and sending them to other parts. Perhaps the metal in the soldier's brain stopped most dream messages.

Why do we dream? Some scientists think that dreams help your brain to arrange, in some useful way, all the ideas, sights, and sounds that come to you during the day.

This map of the brain shows which parts connect to sense receptors. ▶

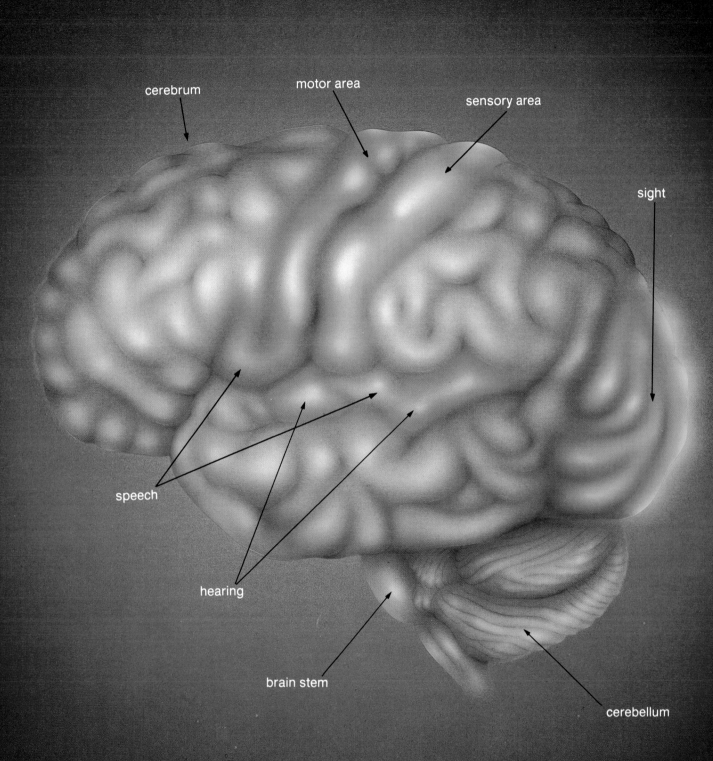

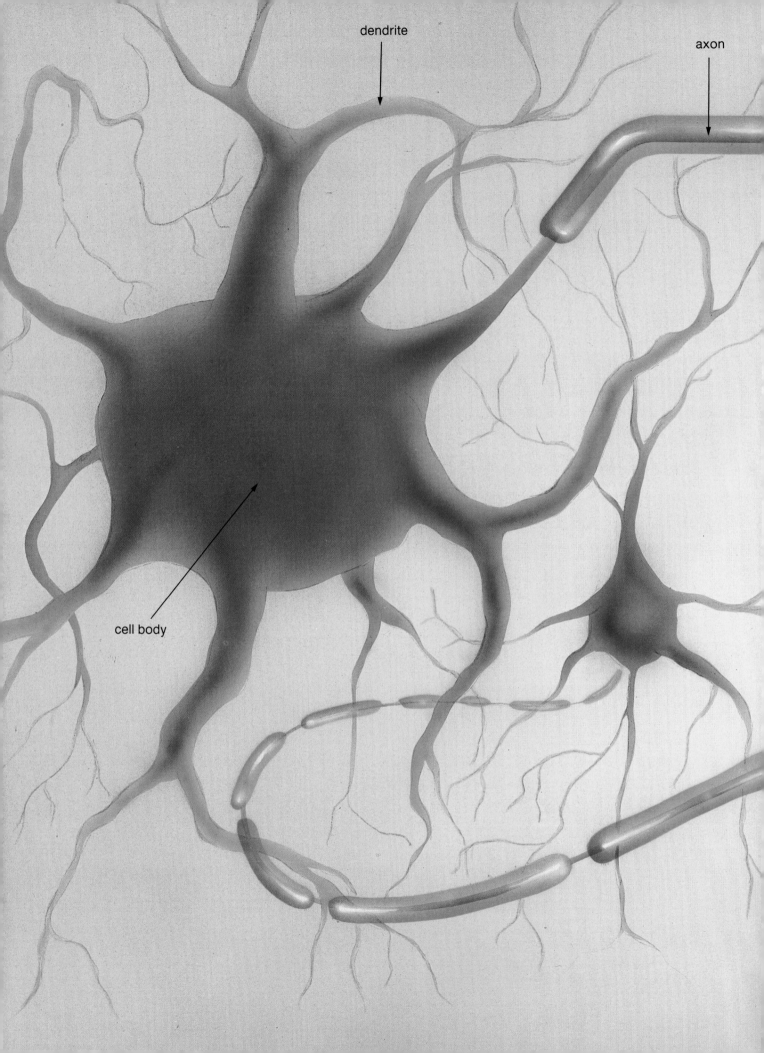

People sometimes even solve problems in their dreams. One well-known scientist tried, while he was awake, to invent an experiment in electricity. No ideas came to him. Then in the middle of the night he woke up, got dressed, and rushed to his laboratory. In a dream he had worked out the whole experiment—correctly!

What about scary dreams and dreams that tell stories? Scientists and doctors still don't know why you have them.

Introducing Your Senses

You see with your eyes and hear with your ears—right? Yes and no. Exactly the same kind of electrical signal goes along nerves from your eyes and from your ears to your brain. But the signals go to different places in the brain. Your eyes and ears are sense organs that collect information; it is really your brain that does the seeing and hearing. The nerves that carry signals to the brain are called sensory nerves.

Each of your sense organs has its own kind of detective cells, known as receptor cells. The receptors pick up clues and start the electrical signals on their way along the sensory nerves to the brain.

Your skin has five main kinds of receptor cells scattered all over your body. They detect heat, cold, light, touch, pressure, and pain. You have the most receptors for pain and the fewest for cold. The remarkable thing is that these five kinds of receptors, or combinations of them, can give you the feel of so many different things, such as slippery soap, sticky glue, rough cement. An itch comes from light-touch receptors with a little help from pain receptors. A tickle is a moving itch.

myelin sheath

synapse

Some neurons are very small. But others are the longest cells in our body.

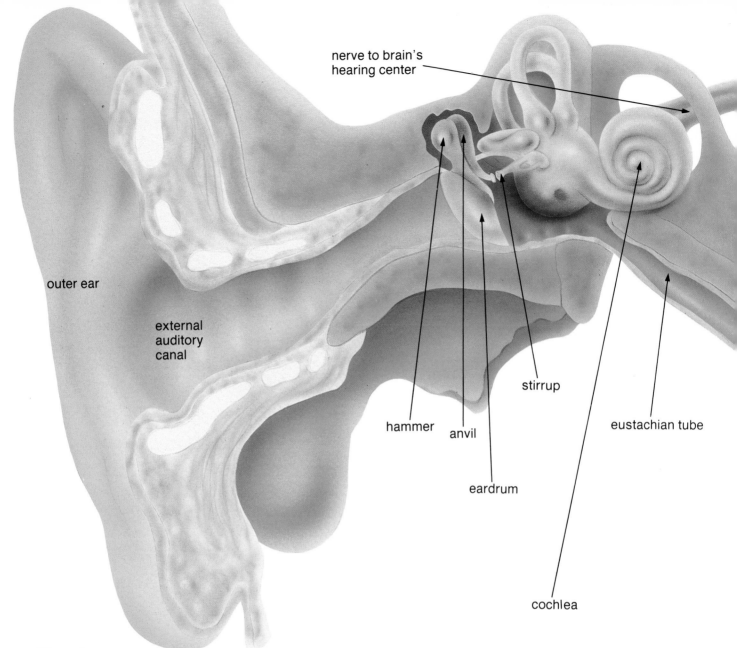

nerve to brain's
hearing center

outer ear

external
auditory
canal

hammer

anvil

stirrup

eardrum

eustachian tube

cochlea

Hearing

"Hello!" says a voice on the telephone. What happens next? Sound waves from the phone receiver enter your ear and make your eardrum vibrate. The vibrations are picked up by three small bones on the inside of the eardrum. The first bone taps against the second bone. It taps against the third, which taps against another drum, called the oval window. The oval window covers an opening in the spiral-shaped chamber of your inner ear. The spiral contains a liquid and is lined with rows of extremely small hair cells. When the oval window is tapped, the liquid jostles the hairs.

Each hair cell is pushed into action by a particular sound vibration. Hair cells at the bottom of the spiral chamber respond best to high sounds. Those at the top respond to low tones. The jostling starts many currents of electricity in nerves that carry messages to the brain. So it takes thousands of waving hairs to bring you that "hello" on the telephone.

Three hollow tubes in your ear called the semicircular canals don't have anything to do with hearing. The canals are filled with liquid, and they have patches of little hair cells. Signals from the hairs travel along sensory nerves to a special part of the brain—the part that controls your sense of balance. When you take a step, the liquid in the tubes moves the hairs. When the brain gets signals from the hairs, it sends out messages along motor nerves. Some messages make certain leg muscles relax. At the same moment other messages tell other leg muscles to contract just the right amount. Muscles in other parts of your body also relax or contract just the right amount. And so you stay in balance for another step.

Seeing

All the parts of your eye, working together, let your brain know what you are seeing. If a computer did the same thing, it would have to make at least 10 billion calculations a second!

Millions of receptor cells make up the retina, which lines the inside of the eye. Some of the cells, shaped like rods, give black-and-

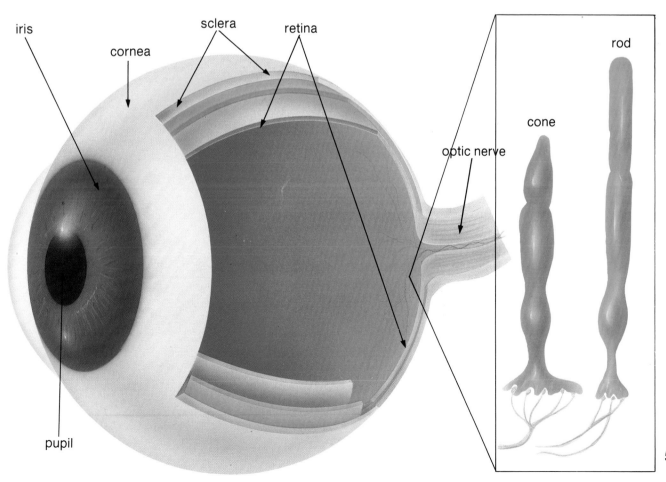

iris

cornea

sclera

retina

rod

cone

optic nerve

pupil

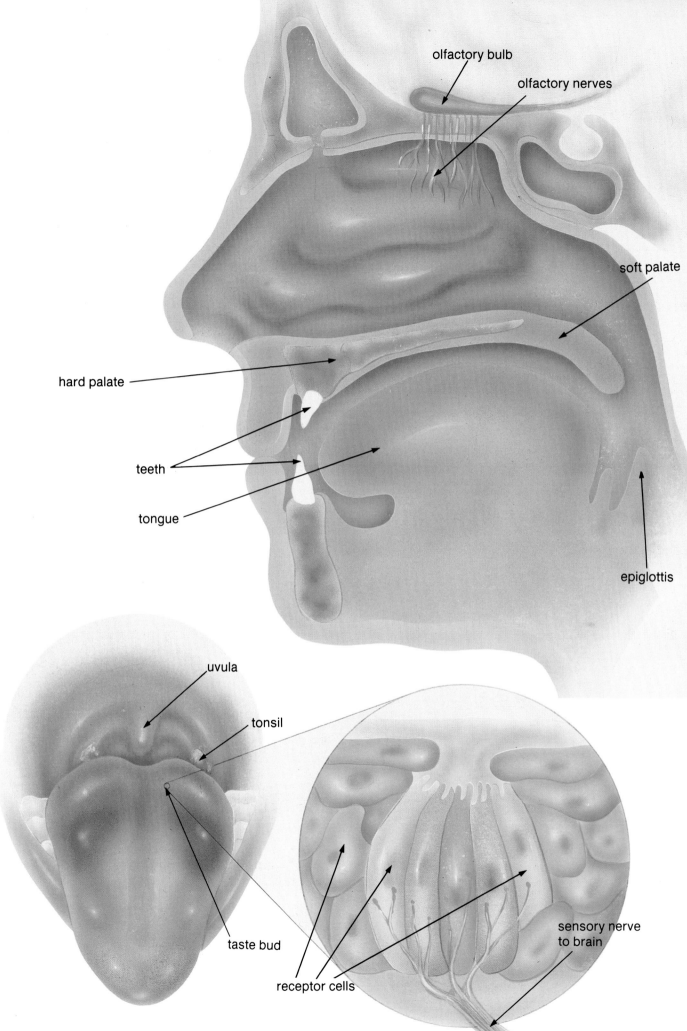

olfactory bulb

olfactory nerves

soft palate

hard palate

teeth

tongue

epiglottis

uvula

tonsil

taste bud

receptor cells

sensory nerve
to brain

white images. The rest, called cones, detect colors. The cornea, a transparent skin covering, protects the inner eye and lets light pass through to the retina. The iris is the colored tissue that surrounds the pupil, which is the opening to the inside of the eye. The lens is a transparent sac of fluid. Muscles attached to the lens change its shape, depending on the distance of the object being looked at. Muscles attached to the outside of the eyeball move the eye up, down, right, and left.

Tasting

Taste receptors are clustered together in bunches that look like tiny heads of garlic. Each cluster is called a taste bud. A batch of about 200 taste buds line the crack around each bump on your tongue. Others are scattered on the roof and back of your mouth. Altogether, you have perhaps 10,000 taste buds.

The buds at the very front of your tongue detect sweet things. The buds just behind these pick up salty tastes. The buds at the sides of the tongue detect sour tastes, and the buds at the back detect bitter ones. The flavors of almost everything you eat are combinations of those four tastes. But, sometimes, taste is also partly smell. When you have a bad cold and a stuffy nose, you can't tell the difference between orange juice and lemonade. Your brain must add together the fruit-smell message from your nose and the sweet-sour messages from your tongue.

Cold foods make your taste buds less sensitive. That is why ice cream tastes much sweeter after it has melted. If you hold an ice cube in your mouth for a while before you take medicine, you won't notice whether the medicine has a bad taste!

Smelling

A smell is something you never forget. Once your nose has detected the odor of popcorn, you will always recognize it when you smell it. Some people have a very keen sense of smell. They can detect odors that are too faint for other people to notice. As a rule, girls are better than boys at this smell detecting.

Your smell receptors are high inside each nostril in a little patch of cells not much bigger than your thumbnail. There are about twenty million receptors in each patch, and every one of them ends in twenty hairlike bristles. It is the tuft of bristles that picks up odors.

The smell of popcorn actually comes from tiny airborne corn particles, but the receptors can't recognize the particles if they are dry. First they have to be dissolved in mucus in the nose. Then the bristles can identify even one molecule. The molecules start the electrical signal that tells the brain "popcorn!"

Skeletal System

When you look at a skeleton, it may seem to be just a collection of stony props to hold up the rest of the body. Actually your bones are living parts of you, busy places where important things happen. Less than half of each of your bones is made of hard minerals. About one-fourth of each bone is water. The rest is living cells and tissue.

A bone cell starts out entirely soft. Gradually it surrounds itself with minerals, but tiny fibers still connect it with other cells and with blood vessels that bring it food and oxygen.

The bones in your arms and legs are called the long bones. The center of the long bones holds a buttery-looking yellow marrow. This contains fat that is stored up in case your body needs extra nourishment. Near their ends, the long bones have spongy areas with spaces where nerves and blood vessels run in and out. The spaces are filled with a tissue called red marrow. Like a factory, the red marrow manufactures blood cells. It turns out vast numbers of red cells, many platelets, and some kinds of white cells. The red cells and platelets soon move into the bloodstream. But some white cells just sit, waiting for an emergency signal to call them out.

Every second, the marrow makes more than two million new red cells, and it can increase production if necessary. Suppose you do a lot of hard pushups. Then your body needs more oxygen. The kidneys detect this, and they squirt a special chemical into the blood. The chemical signals the marrow, "Produce more red cells!" Soon a flock of new red blood cells will be carrying extra oxygen to the hard-working muscle cells.

Your skeleton is more than a bunch of bones.
It is a busy place where important things happen. ▶

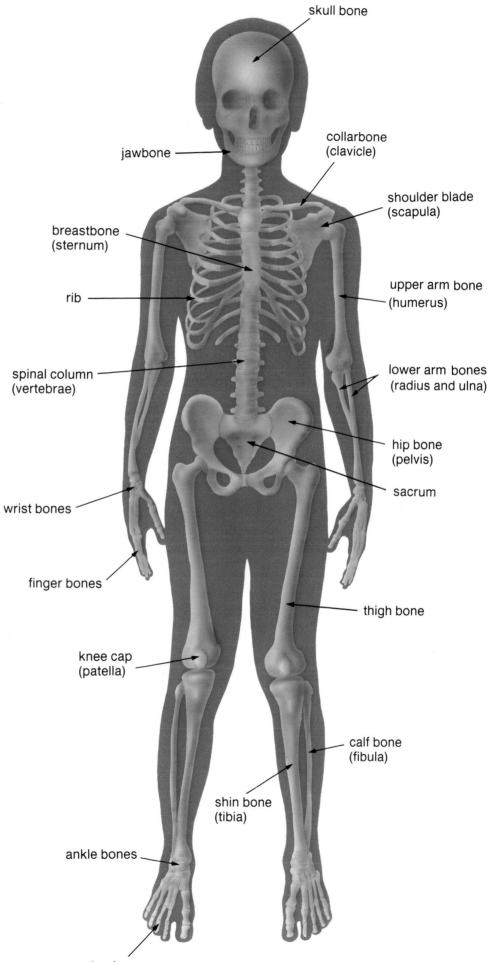

skull bone

jawbone

collarbone
(clavicle)

shoulder blade
(scapula)

breastbone
(sternum)

rib

upper arm bone
(humerus)

spinal column
(vertebrae)

lower arm bones
(radius and ulna)

hip bone
(pelvis)

sacrum

wrist bones

finger bones

thigh bone

knee cap
(patella)

calf bone
(fibula)

shin bone
(tibia)

ankle bones

toe bones

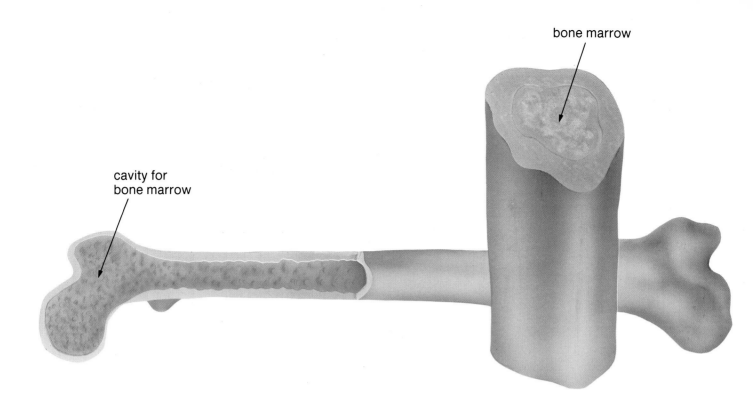

cavity for
bone marrow

bone marrow

The Joints

Your separate bones meet one another at the joints. You have different kinds of joints to take care of all the different motions your body has to make. Strong bands of tissue called ligaments hold the bones together, but not too tightly. The bones move easily at the joints because the ends are covered with smooth cartilage, and a special fluid between the bones keeps the ends oiled.

If you break a bone, it quickly begins to heal itself. On both sides of the break, new bone cells form and start growing toward each other. No one knows exactly why the new bone cells are able to grow in the right direction or what stops their growth when the break is mended. A child's broken bone heals more than five times faster than an adult's.

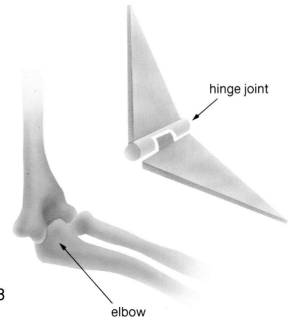

hinge joint

elbow

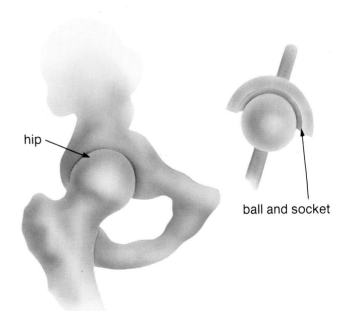

hip

ball and socket

The Backbone

Your backbone is really a column of separate bones called vertebrae. (A single one of these bones is called a vertebra.) You have thirty-three of these separate bones, but as you get older some of them will join or fuse. By the time you are an adult you will have only twenty-six, plus a tailbone. Together with your skull, the vertebrae protect your brain and spinal cord. Between the bones in your back, or spine, lie small disc-shaped pads of cartilage. These discs make it possible for you to bend, and they take up the shock when you walk or jump.

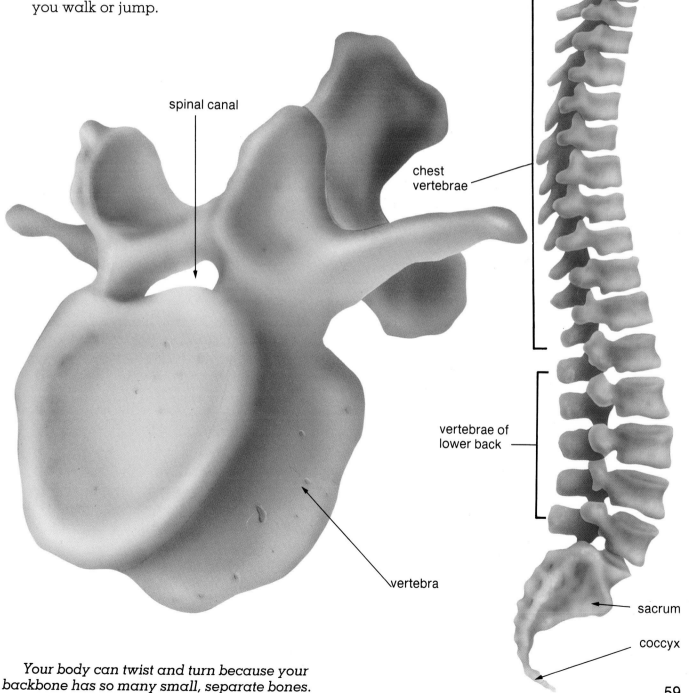

spinal canal

vertebra

neck vertebrae

atlas

axis

chest vertebrae

vertebrae of lower back

sacrum

coccyx

Your body can twist and turn because your backbone has so many small, separate bones.

59

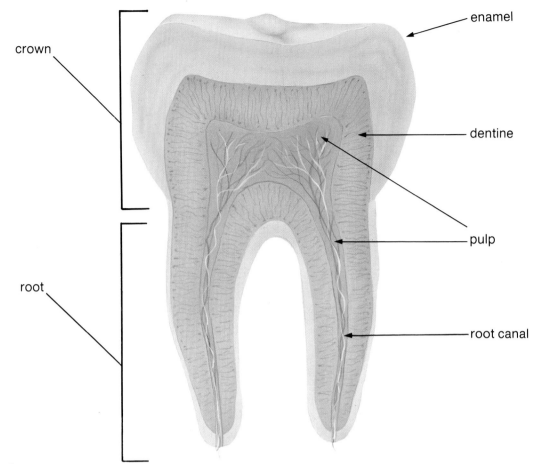

crown

enamel

dentine

pulp

root

root canal

The Teeth

  What's harder than bone? The outside part of a tooth. Under a microscope, this white stuff, called enamel, looks like the six-sided cells of a honeycomb, all fitted closely together. The enamel forms a tight covering that protects the two inside layers of a tooth.

  The middle layer, called dentine, is really a kind of bone, and it is not quite as hard as the enamel. The third layer—the one inside the other two—is the pulp, a soft tissue filled with blood vessels and nerve endings.

  Unlike other bones, dentine cannot repair itself. Neither can enamel. If you get a cavity, no new cells will form in those two outside layers of your tooth. What causes a cavity? The answer is bacteria that live in your mouth. But the bacteria don't eat holes in your teeth. They live on the food that comes into your mouth—especially sugar. While bacteria are digesting sugar, they produce an acid, and the acid dissolves the hard minerals in teeth.

  If a cavity goes all the way through the enamel and the dentine into the pulp, you will soon know the bad news. Nerve endings in the pulp will send out pain signals, and unless the cavity is filled, the tooth will hurt until the pulp finally dies. This means the whole tooth is dead, and sooner or later it will break apart or drop out. No wonder people tell you to brush your teeth, especially after eating anything sweet!

You were born with only little buds of teeth in your jaws. Before you were six years old, the buds turned into a set of twenty baby teeth, sometimes called milk teeth. As you get older, your jaws grow larger, with space for new teeth that fill the gaps left when the baby teeth fall out.

Some of your second teeth will grow more slowly than others. But, by the time you are twenty-one, you should have all or most of the thirty-two teeth in your permanent set.

It's a fact that . . .

- What makes your teeth sprout is a mystery. Dentists used to think that teeth developed from roots in the jaw. But scientists then discovered that the tips of the teeth, called the crowns, grow outward even when they are separated from their roots. Some dentists now believe that a hormone gives signals for teeth to grow—but that theory has not yet been proven.

- You are taller in space than on Earth. In space, gravity does not pull you down. So your bones can spread apart a little at the joints, and you are as much as half an inch taller.

- Sometimes a bone isn't really a bone. The funny bone is a nerve that lies close to a bone in your elbow.

- Your smallest bone is in your ear. Your largest bone is in your thigh.

Muscular System

Have you ever watched a big league baseball player pitch? The muscles that move the pitcher's bones are marvelous, complex bundles of cells and fibers. Yet they work in a very simple way. All they do is tighten up—that is, contract—and relax. Of course, the pitcher doesn't tell each separate muscle what to do. He just decides to throw, and his brain does the rest.

Striped Muscles

The muscles that work for the pitcher are bundles of long, thin cells called striped muscle cells. Each muscle cell can contract and relax.

You have two sets of muscles attached to many of your bones. To open your mouth, for example, one set pulls your jaw down. When you close your mouth, that set of muscles relaxes and the other set contracts to pull your jaw up. Even when you are just sitting still, some of your muscle cells are exercising slightly. They take turns contracting and relaxing a few at a time. This means your muscles are in good condition—that they have good muscle tone.

The nerves that carry electrical messages from your brain to your striped muscles are motor nerves. Each motor nerve ends in little pads. When the electric current reaches them, the pads squirt out a chemical, and that puts the muscle to work.

62

The Muscle System

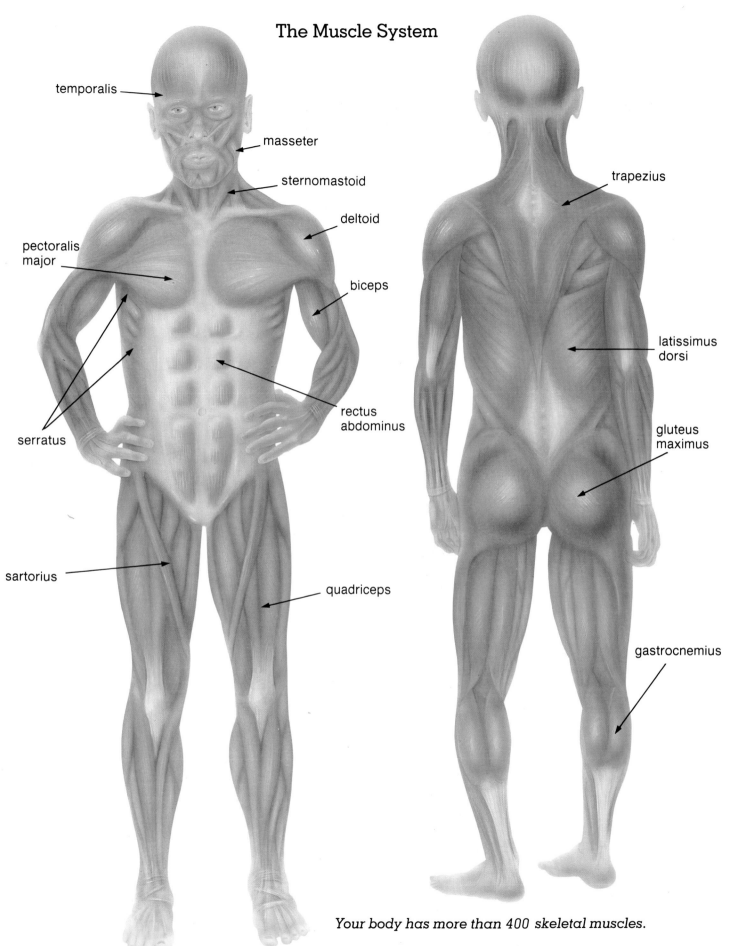

temporalis

masseter

sternomastoid

deltoid

pectoralis major

biceps

serratus

rectus abdominus

sartorius

quadriceps

trapezius

latissimus dorsi

gluteus maximus

gastrocnemius

Your body has more than 400 skeletal muscles.

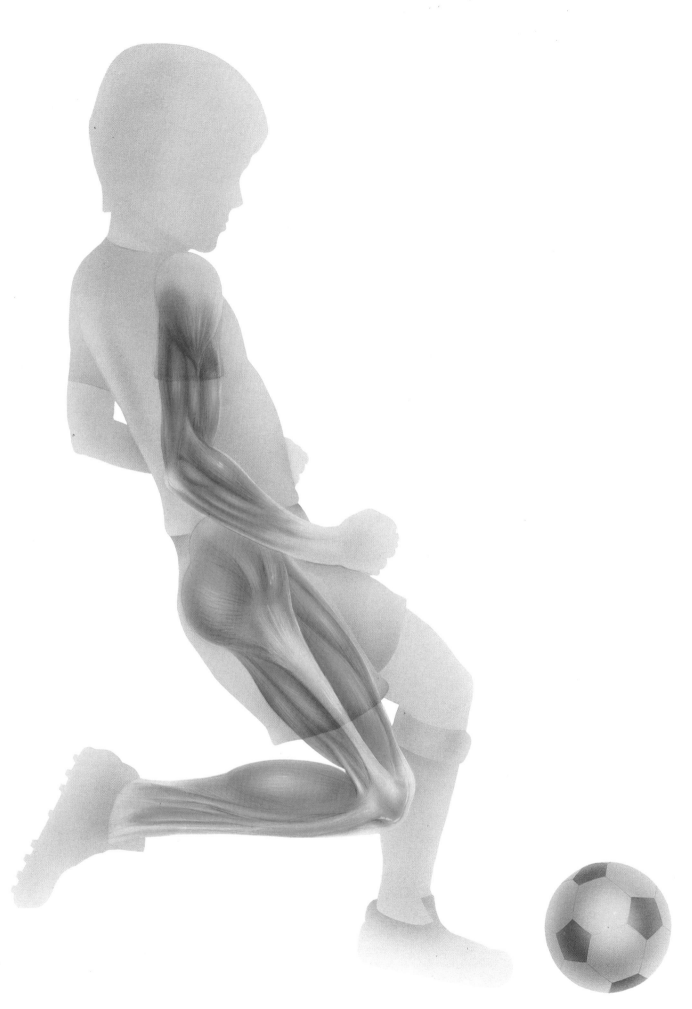

Heart Muscle

Your heart is made of striped muscle cells, but they are a special kind. They have fewer stripes than the striped muscle cells in the rest of your body, and they are very strong. They need to be strong to keep your heart pumping through your whole life.

Smooth Muscles

Smooth muscles have no stripes at all, and they are not attached to bone. They are the muscles in the walls of your intestines and bladder, your esophagus, and your blood vessels. Scientists call them involuntary muscles because you don't make a decision to move them. They are controlled by a part of your brain that keeps them working automatically. You never have to wonder whether the pulse in your arteries is throbbing. And you can always be sure that the wavelike motion of the intestines is sending digested food along.

It's a fact that . . .

• Your tongue is made up of many groups of muscles, which is why you can move it in many directions and move it quickly. As you chew, you push food around in your mouth with your tongue. When you are ready to swallow food, your tongue rises against the roof of your mouth and spreads against the sides. In this way the food is pushed into your pharynx.

• Some people's tongues are so flexible they can be rolled into the shape of a tube!

• Your tongue is important in helping to form words when you talk. Try to say the word "language" without using your tongue!

• When you smile, frown, or make a funny face, you use your facial muscles to pull the skin on your face into the right position.

• A round muscle called a sphincter surrounds your mouth. You use it for kissing, drinking through a straw, and saying "oh."

• There is a good reason why you shiver when you feel cold. Your body senses a drop in temperature and automatically causes small groups of your muscles to contract one after another. All this activity of your muscles warms you up!

Stretch! Bend! Kick! The cells in muscles contract and relax when nerves bring them messages from the brain.

Endocrine System

After scientists discovered that electric currents carry messages to and from the brain, they still had questions. Do secret messengers operate in the body? If so, which one tells the kidneys, "There is too much salt in the blood"? What makes a frightened person's heart beat faster? Does that same messenger notify bone cells to grow? Finally, the mystery was solved. There are many different messengers, and they are all chemicals called hormones.

Where do hormones come from? One by one, scientific detectives traced them back to various groups of cells called glands. Some glands were already known—tear glands, mucus glands, stomach acid glands. All of these produce liquids that pour out through tiny tubes to places where they are needed—in the eye, in the nose, in the stomach. But glands that produce hormones are different. They have no tubes. Instead, they empty their chemicals directly into the blood. And the blood carries these chemicals everywhere in the body. The hormone makers are called endocrine glands.

There are more than a dozen endocrine glands. But one of them, the pituitary, is called "the master," because it regulates the others. Hormones from the pituitary move through the bloodstream to each of the other glands, telling them when to send out their own chemical messengers. One of the pituitary hormones is the growth hormone. It controls how much and how fast you grow. To do this, it turns on and off the amount of nourishment that your cells can take in.

When girls and boys become teenagers—and sometimes even a year or two before that—growth hormones cause changes in the way they grow. A girl's arms and legs become more rounded. A boy may grow several inches taller in just a few months. The growth hormone is responsible for these changes. At the same time, another pituitary hormone takes messages to the sex glands.

In a girl the sex glands are the ovaries. Hormones from the pituitary and the ovaries cause her breasts to develop. Her skin and hair become a little darker. She begins to have hair under her arms and between her legs at the top of her thighs. At this time, the ovaries begin to produce fully developed egg cells. You'll find out more about them in the next chapter.

A boy's sex glands are the testes, and their hormones have two different tasks. First, they cause changes that make him look more like a man. Hair begins to grow on his face and chest, under his arms, and between his legs at the top of his thighs. His voice becomes deeper. The testes also manufacture special male cells called sperm cells. You'll find out more about them, too, in the next chapter.

This time of change in young people is called adolescence. You can think of it as a sort of bridge. On one side of the bridge you are a child. On the other side you are grown up and can have children of your own.

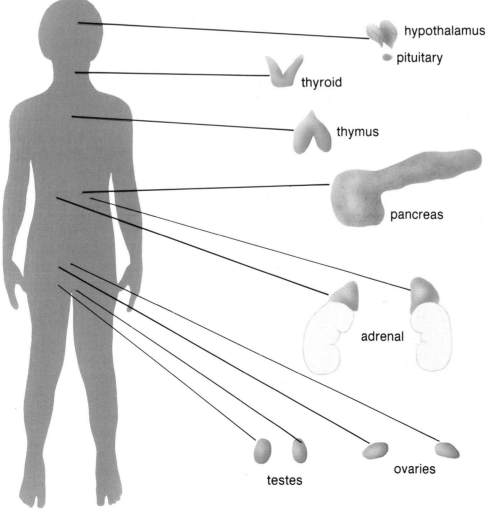

hypothalamus

pituitary

thyroid

thymus

pancreas

adrenal

testes

ovaries

Endocrine glands release hormones into the blood. These chemicals control many of your body's activities. They also affect your feelings.

Reproductive System

Thousands of years ago, people knew that a baby always has both a mother and a father. But no one knew exactly how the baby grew inside the mother's body. At last, only about 140 years ago, scientists discovered what happens first. One of the father's sperm cells joins one of the mother's egg cells, forming a fertilized egg cell.

The egg cell, or ovum, is the only cell in the body that is large enough to see without a microscope. It is about as big around as the tip of a needle. The sperm is much smaller, but both cells have a nucleus and the other usual cell parts. Remember, the nucleus is very important because it directs what the other parts of the cell do.

The nucleus of every cell you've read about so far contains forty-six little threads called chromosomes. Scientists now know that the sperm and ovum are different. Each of them has only twenty-three chromosomes. But after the sperm and ovum join, forming a single fertilized egg cell, their combined chromosomes add up to the right number—that is, forty-six.

At first, the two sets of threadlike chromosomes are tangled together in the new cell's nucleus. Then, after a few hours, each thread splits in two, from end to end. Next, one half of each thread from the mother's ovum pairs up with one half of a thread from the father's sperm. Now the fertilized cell is ready to divide and start the process of growing into a baby.

The Reproductive System

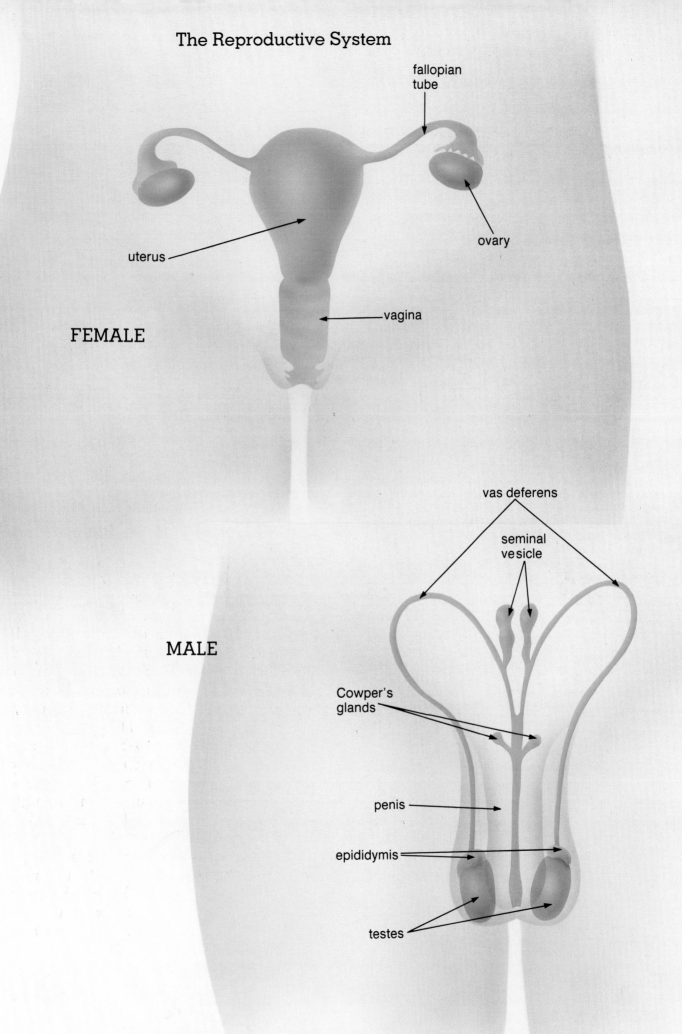

fallopian
tube

ovary

uterus

vagina

FEMALE

vas deferens

seminal
vesicle

Cowper's
glands

penis

epididymis

testes

MALE

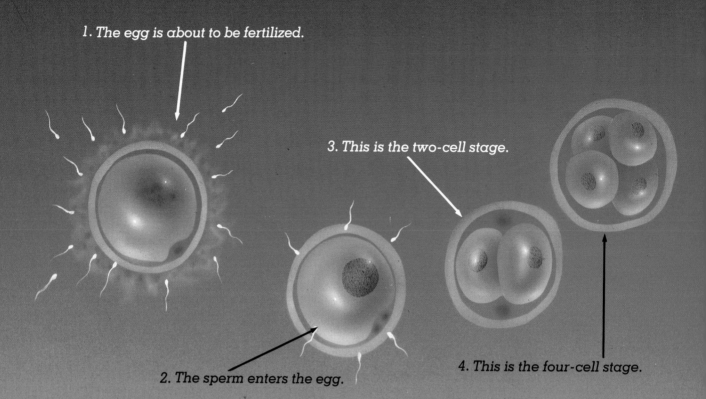

1. *The egg is about to be fertilized.*

3. *This is the two-cell stage.*

2. *The sperm enters the egg.*

4. *This is the four-cell stage.*

Girl or Boy?

Will the baby be a girl or a boy? At first, a cluster of cells that will become a girl looks exactly like a cluster that will become a boy. More cells develop, and they form what is called the embryo. When the embryo is about six weeks old, it will begin to show that it has either male or female sex organs.

Still, the question "girl or boy?" was actually answered at the moment the sperm entered the ovum. And the answer depended on those threads called chromosomes. An ovum always has one special chromosome called the X chromosome. But sperm cells are not so dependable. Some sperm cells have the X chromosome, and some have a different one called the Y chromosome. Now what happens when two sets of chromosomes are paired together in the fertilized egg cell? This is the way one scientist, Dr. Alex Novikoff, explains it:

X (from Mother) + X (from Father) = XX (Girl)
X (from Mother) + Y (from Father) = XY (Boy)

What decides whether a sperm with an X chromosome or a sperm with a Y chromosome joins the ovum? The scientist says it's "just luck!"

These are the later stages.

When this process of cell division is finished, a new human being will have been created.

Twins and Triplets

Long, long ago, when some people believed in witches, the birth of twins was sometimes called a bad luck sign for the parents. But other people believed that the birth of twins was a sign of good luck. Of course, it was neither. This is what really happens: Sometimes the fertilized cell splits into two completely separate parts when it divides just after the sperm joins the ovum. The parts are almost exactly alike, and each becomes an embryo. Both embryos will be either male or female. Twins formed in this way are called identical twins.

Sometimes, two different egg cells are fertilized by two different sperm cells at about the same time. When these form embryos, one may be a girl, the other a boy, or both may be of the same sex. But they are not exactly alike. They are called fraternal twins because they are really just ordinary sisters or brothers who happened to be born at the same time.

Triplets can be a combination. Two of them may be identical twins, and the third may come from a separate fertilized egg. Or all three may grow from one fertilized egg cell.

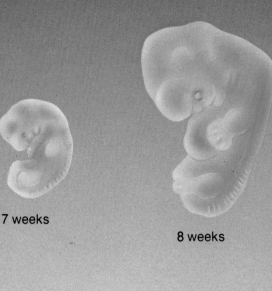

7 weeks

8 weeks

6 weeks

9 weeks

5 weeks

Who Does Baby Look Like?

Sometimes a baby will have curly hair like its father and brown eyes like its mother. Maybe its nose and ears are like its father's, too. Why? The answer is again chromosomes.

Chromosomes look like strings of tiny beads. The beads are called genes, and there are thousands of them. Each gene produces an enzyme that puts chemicals to work in the growing embryo. The genes direct the formation of all body parts, including hair type, eye color, shape of nose and ears. Remember, a baby gets some genes from the twenty-three chromosomes in the ovum and some from the twenty-three chromosomes in the sperm. When the chromosomes split and pair up, the genes get jumbled around. So a child will receive some genes from the mother and some from the father. That is why children can have features like those of one or both parents.

How Did Baby Get Here?

Where did the sperm and ovum get their start? First look at the drawing of a man's reproductive organs. (They are called reproductive organs because they help produce another human being.) Millions and millions of sperm cells are made in the testes. Sperm cells are the only cells that can move by themselves. They have a long

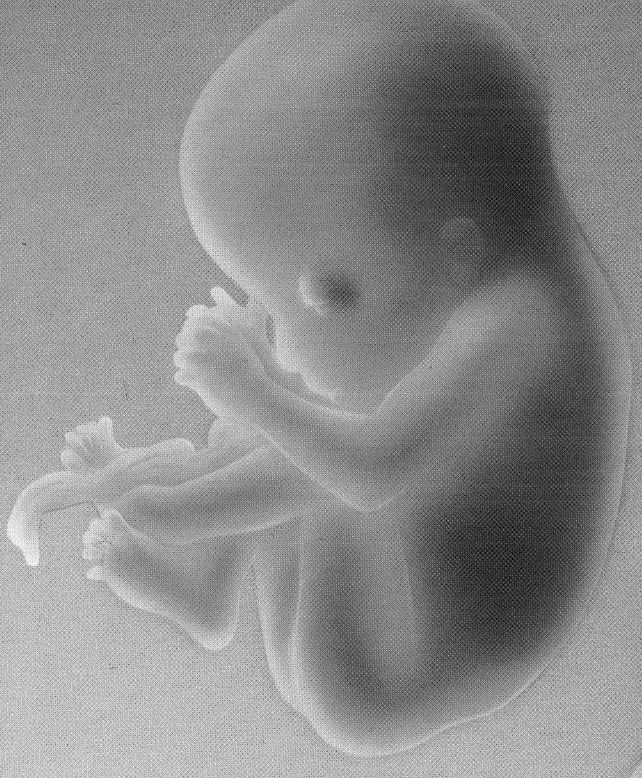

16 weeks

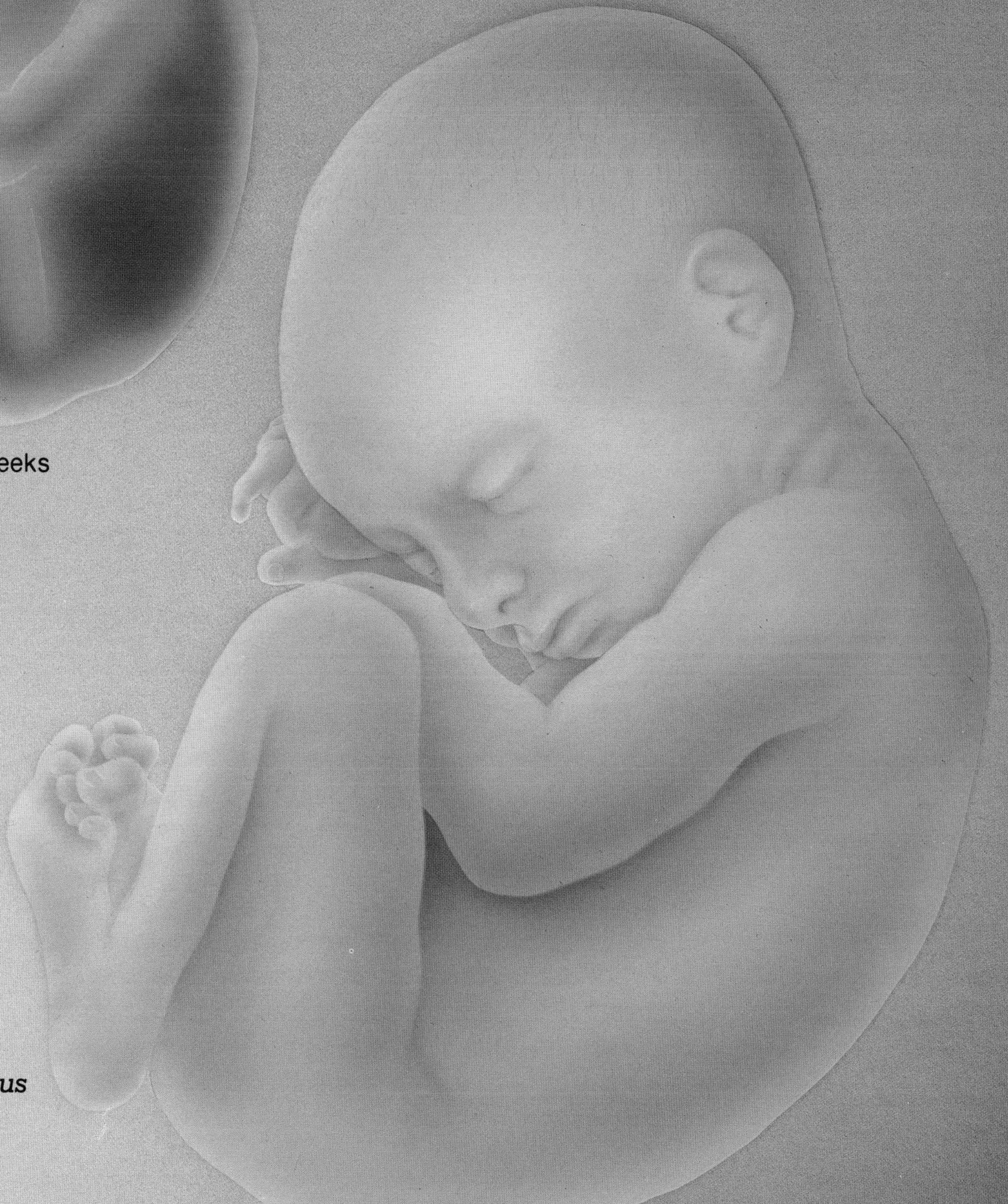

In an embryo, the
skeletal and nervous
systems form first.
Then the digestive
and circulatory
systems form.

9 months

way to travel from the testes, up through a curving tube, and then down through the penis. On the way they are bathed in fluids from several glands. The fluids protect them as they swim with a whiplike motion of the tail.

The penis is usually soft and flexible. But when a man and woman lie close together, with loving thoughts and touches, the penis stiffens. Now the man can fit it into the opening of a tube called the vagina, which is in the woman's body. Movement of the penis causes muscles in and around it to tighten. This tightening pushes sperm cells out of the man's body into the vagina. There the journey of the sperm cells continues.

Now look at the picture of a woman's reproductive organs. The two ovaries hold the egg cells. About once every four weeks, a small bump rises on the outside of one of the ovaries. The bump breaks open, and out comes an egg cell—an ovum. At the same time the fingerlike ends of a Fallopian tube reach toward the cell, and draw it into the tube.

The Fallopian tube is the place where the ovum and the sperm cells usually meet. Many sperm cells have been moving steadily from the vagina, up through a sac called the uterus. Thousands of the sperm reach the Fallopian tube. But only one enters the ovum. The moment it does so, a chemical change happens, and no other sperm can get in.

An Embryo Forms

This fertilized cell divides several times and forms an embryo. Then it leaves the tube and comes down into the uterus. There the embryo attaches itself to the soft uterus wall and keeps on growing. Soon it makes a wrapping for itself called the placenta. Blood vessels in the placenta lie close to blood vessels in the uterus wall. So food and oxygen pass from the mother's blood into the placenta and then through a tube called the umbilical cord to the growing embryo. As the embryo grows, it produces wastes. These pass through the umbilical cord and placenta into the mother's blood. Then they are removed along with the mother's own wastes.

While the embryo is growing inside the placenta in the uterus, it is always in touch with the mother. Every moment for about nine months it changes and develops. The more it grows, the more the walls of the uterus stretch to hold it. Finally, when special hormones signal it is time, the walls of the vagina also stretch. The muscles in the uterus contract. And a new life is pushed into the world.

One last thing—the umbilical cord—connects a new baby to the place where it was developing for nine months. The placenta, with the cord, is also pushed out of the mother's uterus. Now the baby is breathing on its own and no longer needs the cord, so it is snipped off. Still, a reminder of it is left. The tiny stump of the cord is the navel—the belly button.

That ends our story about the human body. It is a story of parts working together in almost unbelievably complex ways, but in harmony. It is also a story that hasn't been finished. Many puzzles about the body still wait to be solved. But almost every day a scientific detective can say: "At last! We have the answer to one more mystery. Case closed!"

It's a fact that . . .

• Some people in the 1800s had a strange idea about how a baby develops. They thought that a sperm cell contained a whole, tiny person. This miniature person was called a homunculus, which means "little man." A mother's ovum was thought of as merely a convenient place where the homunculus could grow. One fake scientist even claimed he had seen a "little man" with his microscope!

• Identical twins are born once in about every 270 births. Fraternal twins are born once in about every 100 births. Triplets are born once in about 7,569 births, quadruplets once in about 658,503 births, and quintuplets once in about 57,289,761 births.

• Identical twins look very much alike. They have eyes and hair of the same color and eyebrows of the same shape. Often the friends and teachers of identical twins have difficulty telling them apart. Even the twins' fingerprints and the prints on the soles of their feet are almost identical.

Glossary

Adolescence (ad LES nts) The time of life when girls' and boys' bodies change and develop the characteristics of adults.

Allergy (all AR jee) Extreme physical reaction to some substances that causes sneezing, itching, or other discomforts.

Alveoli (al VEE eh lee) Tiny sacs at the ends of tubes that bring air into the lungs.

Antibody A molecule of a chemical that certain white blood cells produce. Antibodies help to get rid of viruses and other substances that don't belong in the body.

Arteries The blood vessels that carry blood from the heart to other parts of the body.

Bile A yellowish liquid produced by the liver. Bile contains chemicals that help digest food, and is stored in a sac called the gallbladder.

Bronchi (BRONG kee) Two short, fat tubes that connect the windpipe with the lungs.

Capillaries Blood vessels that connect arteries with veins.

Cartilage A tough tissue that forms the ears, the tip of the nose, and the ends of the ribs. It also covers the ends of bones where they come together at joints.

Cell The smallest complete part of the body, each cell is made up of a jell-like substance enclosed in a cell wall. Cells are sometimes called the body's building blocks. Each cell contains several parts; among them are the nucleus, mitochondria, ribosomes, lysosomes, and vacuoles. Each part has a special job to do.

Cerebrum (seh REE brem) The part of the brain that covers almost all the other parts. This is where learning, thinking, remembering, and making decisions goes on.

Chromosomes (KRO meh zomes) Tiny strings of material inside the nucleus of a cell. The nucleus of most human cells contains 46 chromosomes. Each chromosome is divided into sections called genes.

Cornea   The clear skin that covers and protects the inner eye.

Embryo   The group of cells that develops from a fertilized egg cell. For about nine months, the embryo continues to grow and develop into a baby.

Enzyme   (EN zime) A chemical in the body that can break big molecules into smaller molecules. Some enzymes help to digest food. Others, such as those in tears, help prevent infection.

Epidermis   (ep uh DER mes) The outermost part of the skin, made up of two layers of cells.

Esophagus   (ee SAHF uh gus) The tube that carries food from the throat to the stomach.

Follicle   (FOL eh kul) A small bag in the skin. Hair cells grow from follicles.

Hemoglobin   (HE me glo bin) A chemical in red blood cells that gives the cells their color.

Larynx   (LAR inks) The voice box in the upper part of the windpipe at the front of the throat. It is protected by a band of cartilage called the Adam's apple.

Lymph   (LIMpf) A colorless fluid that bathes the body's cells. It is formed from part of the blood that seeps through the capillary walls. Lymph contains the same minerals that are found in sea water.

Mitochondria   (mite eh KAHN dree ah) The parts of cells that change food into energy.

Neurons   Cells that make up the brain and nerves.

Nucleus   The part of a cell that directs the activities of other parts. Most cells have a nucleus. New red blood cells are made with a nucleus but lose it when they go to work in the blood.

Organ   Groups of tissues, doing the same job, make up the organs of the body. The eyes, the stomach, and kidneys are some of the body's organs.

Ovaries   The two organs in a woman's body that produce egg cells.

Placenta   (pla SEN te) An envelope of tissues that lines the inside of a mother's uterus while a baby is developing there.

Plasma   The yellowish liquid part of the blood.

Sperm cell   The male cell that can move by itself. When it joins with a female egg cell, they form a fertilized egg cell from which a baby develops.

Testes   (TES teez) The male sex organs that produce sperm cells and male sex hormones.

Tissue   A large group of cells, all of the same kind, that work together. Several kinds of tissue, doing the same job, make up an organ.

Umbilical cord   (um BILL eh kull) A tube that connects the mother's body to the developing embryo.

Veins   The blood vessels that carry blood back to the heart after it has been pumped through the arteries and capillaries.

Index

Page numbers in *italic type* refer to information that goes with illustrations.

J 6/13 Lu 10/12 ZZ circ 14 lu